Praise for *Fearless Growth*:

"Amanda Setili's *Fearless Growth* strikes at the essence of what it takes to operate and grow successfully in fast-changing markets: agility. Sharing insights from Lyft, Apple, Facebook, and others, Setili provides new rules that empower business leaders to surmount any challenge."

—Dr. Marcell Vollmer, Chief Digital Officer, SAP Ariba

"To stay relevant in times of rapid market change, we need to be able to see around corners, and to constantly reinvent ourselves. The largest, most successful companies today—Airbnb, Amazon, Apple, Google, Facebook and others—have built vibrant ecosystems, in which many players create and consume value, in a dynamic and self-reinforcing way. Amanda Setili's book is a brilliant guide to help any company make the strategic shift to a new model for growth, powered by constant innovation, rich partnerships, co-creation with customers and unleashing of employee talent."

—Eli Rosner, Chief Technology Officer, NCR

"Setili provides a powerful set of principles to drive your business to faster and more predictable growth."

—Andy Bodea, Chief Global Operations Officer, Equifax

"Amanda Setili's new rules for fearless growth are spot on. When we trust our employees and foster their intrinsic motivation, when we enable productive debate and the free flow of ideas, we can achieve remarkable growth, even in turbulent times."

—Amy Edmondson, author of *Building the Future* and Professor of Leadership and Management, Harvard Business School

"Setili has created a roadmap that demonstrates how businesses can grow in today's changing economy, leverage their talent, assets and technology, and enhance agility within their team."
—Brian Caldarelli, Chief Financial Officer, PSCU

"Achieving growth in a fast-changing marketplace requires constant innovation. Sometimes that means engaging and serving customers in new ways, developing new revenue streams with partners, or simply making your core business more adaptive and flexible. *Fearless Growth* opens a much-needed window on this exciting new world. Amanda Setili has engagingly provided a pragmatic framework to understand the new levers needed for today's business leaders to achieve manageable, healthy growth."
William "Woody" Faulk, vice president of Innovation & New Ventures, Chick-fil-A, Inc.

FEARLESS GROWTH

GROWTH

The New Rules
to Stay Competitive, Foster
Innovation, and Dominate
Your Markets

AMANDA SETILI

FOREWORD BY MARSHALL GOLDSMITH

CAREER
PRESS

FEARLESS GROWTH
TYPESET BY PERFECTYPE, NASHVILLE, TENNESSEE
Cover design by Howard Grossman/12E Design
Background cover image by Wutip/Envato Elements
Printed in the U.S.A.

To order this title, please call toll-free 1-800-CAREER-1 (NJ and Canada: 201-848-0310) to order using VISA or MasterCard, or for further information on books from Career Press.

The Career Press, Inc.
12 Parish Drive
Wayne, NJ 07470
www.careerpress.com

Library of Congress Cataloging-in-Publication

CIP Data Available Upon Request.

To my mom, Nancy Krueger Keahey, who inspires me daily.

CONTENTS

FOREWORD

In *Fearless Growth*, Amanda Setili addresses the major dilemmas that organizations and leaders are facing today. She provides us with a rulebook for successfully and, more importantly, boldly navigating challenges such as innovation, disruption, and stretched resources.

These issues that Amanda addresses are new and unknown, and can cause significant stress and anxiety, even fear. You may be facing some of these challenges in your own organization. My guess is that if you are in business, you are. And I'd speculate that you probably find that it's a bit scary stepping into the unknown. In this book, you'll find help with this. Amanda will guide you to address such challenges confidently and without fear.

The first step is acknowledging that fear is natural, but not necessary. Says Amanda, "When the ground is shifting beneath your feet, with rapid changes in customer needs, technology, regulations, and the like, you need to act fast. You need to be adaptable, ready for anything. You need to innovate and invest in new lines of business that will fuel future growth." This is hard to do when you are frozen in a panic! So, how do you get out of the fear?

Amanda shows you how. She illustrates, through examples, how large organizations are successfully navigating the new economy, exactly what they do, and how you can do it too. This is a critically important message coming to you at just the right time.

Read Amanda's book, study it, learn it backward and forward, and you'll find that you can navigate even the greatest challenges boldly and fearlessly!

Life is good.

Marshall Goldsmith
The international best-selling author and editor of 36 books including *What Got You Here Won't Get You There* and *Triggers*

PREFACE

In my consulting work at Setili & Associates, I've worked with companies large and small, providing focused advice about their strategic direction. Although every client has unique capabilities and challenges, there is a common struggle for all. How do they grow their business and profitability in these days of rapid changes in technology and customer expectations?

My new book, *Fearless Growth*, will help you answer that question for yourself, and also explore other tough questions about your business. The ability to grow sales and profitability is paramount. When you feel hampered by your perceived limitations, it's easy to fall into stagnant patterns that allow only for slow growth. I'll walk you through illustrations of companies, across many industries, that grew big based on these new rules of growth. You'll be much better equipped to tackle any disruption in your field with boldness and confidence.

Ready to embrace fearless growth? Let's get started.

Fearless Growth

In February 2017, news agency Reuters revealed GM's plans to test thousands of self-driving electric Bolt vehicles in 2018.[1] GM's ultimate goal, which most of us would have had trouble imagining 15 years ago, is to develop a fleet of self-driving vehicles that can be summoned on demand via ride-sharing services.

For GM, the tests are about more than just building customer acceptance. GM will also improve its technology by having the cars collect driving and traffic data from traffic lights, cameras, road sensors, and parking meters.

GM is not the only company racing toward an autonomous-vehicle future. In February 2017, Ford announced that it would invest $1 billion dollars throughout a five-year period in Argo AI, a Pittsburgh-based company with top leadership from Carnegie Mellon, Google, and Uber.[2] Daimler, the parent company of Mercedes-Benz, is teaming up with Uber. Tesla is equipping every car it sells with equipment capable of being remotely upgraded as self-driving capabilities evolve, and other auto companies have their own plans underway.

The GM example demonstrates how big companies can move fast and fearlessly when they want to. Although it may be several more years before government regulators allow fleets of truly driverless vehicles to ply American roads and byways, GM decided that to stay relevant and build a foundation for its future growth, it needed to act *now*.

Why Fearless Growth Is Imperative

When you are in the midst of a fast-changing business environment, as automakers now are, it's easy to let the risks and uncertainty slow you to a crawl. Customer behaviors and preferences are shifting quickly. Technology is accelerating. Competitors are moving fast. The regulatory environment is highly uncertain. The future is difficult to predict or plan for.

Taking the auto sector as an example, we see that consumer values and habits concerning transportation have changed more in the last five years than in the last 50 years. When I was growing up, teens wanted their driver's licenses the day they turned 16. Having a car meant independence, freedom, friends, adventure, privacy, and power. Surprisingly, only about 27 percent of 16-year-olds in the United States today have their license.[3] And all around the world, the trend is similar: People begin driving later, or not at all. What's driving this change in driving habits? When asked why they had not yet gotten a driver's license, 57 percent of non-driving 18- and 19-year-olds said they were "too busy,"[4] and 22 percent said they did not intend to get a license—*ever.*[5]

What?! A teenager who does not intend to get a driver's license? Ever? This would have been unthinkable a generation ago. Needless to say, this trend has the automotive industry worried—*very* worried.

Americans currently spend more than $2 trillion each year on products and services related to car ownership, everything from purchasing the vehicles themselves, to spare tires, oil changes, insurance, auto finance, repairs, and so on. Fewer drivers translates into lower profits for these companies.

Ride-sharing services such as Uber and Lyft, and car-sharing services like Zipcar, car2go, Turo, and BMW's ReachNow service, have made car ownership an option, not a necessity. Daniel Ammann, president of GM, summarized the shift he sees: "There are large groups of customers out there that want to have the convenience and access to a car when they need it, but don't want to have the hassle of ownership."[6]

When the ground is shifting beneath your feet, with rapid changes in customer needs, technology, regulations, and the like, you need to act fast. You need to be adaptable, ready for anything. You need to innovate and invest in new lines of business that will fuel future growth.

It's not always easy to act quickly. Your board and investors expect steady revenue growth and consistent profitability. Your employees are accustomed to doing things the way they've always been done. Even your customers may balk at rapid change, rejecting opportunities to try new products, or to do things in new ways. The core business, which you may have built over many decades, still needs to be run in an efficient and reliable manner. There is little time and limited money to invest in new avenues for revenue growth.

The tension between doing what you are good at—what you know how to do well—and charting new territory is profound. We avoid admitting fear in a corporate setting, but it's reasonable, rational, and natural to be fearful when your core business is under threat of disruption, when customer attitudes are changing at an extraordinary pace, or when you cannot predict or control the changes in your business environment.

Although it is natural to be fearful, it is not necessary. In fact, by following the new rules that I share in the chapters that follow, you can grow boldly and fearlessly.

Five Strategic Dilemmas That Have Become More Acute

GM's moves into autonomous vehicles illustrate how one company, GM, addressed five strategic dilemmas that I've observed countless companies wrestle with. Each of them can result in worry, stress, tension, or even fear.

Strategic Dilemma #1: Should we disrupt our own business before someone else does, or focus on protecting and preserving it? GM's investment in autonomous vehicles is clearly at odds with its historic goal of selling more cars. The company is effectively investing to *reduce* the number of cars on the road. But by getting out in front of the autonomous vehicle trend, and learning as fast as possible, company leaders know that they will be more likely to succeed in the long term, no matter what the future brings.

Strategic Dilemma #2: How much of our scarce attention and resources should we invest in long-term bets, as opposed to meeting the short-term demands of running our business? Though GM has been researching autonomous vehicles for years, the company accelerated its strategy in 2016, investing $500 million in ride-sharing company Lyft in January, and acquiring three-year-old, 40-employee (at the time of acquisition) Cruise Automation later that year for $581 million. GM's strategy is to move first and fast in bringing autonomous vehicles into the ride-sharing arena, targeting urban areas with young populations likely to be comfortable with the idea of autonomous ride-sharing. The $1 billion dollars is a significant investment for GM, but investing in Lyft and Cruise Automation is not a bet-the-company move. The investment, which amounts to only about 2 percent of its total market capitalization, allows GM to test the waters, and enables the company to be on the learning frontier of car-sharing and self-driving cars. Meanwhile, GM has a range of other programs to support incremental growth in its core business.

Strategic Dilemma #3: To what extent should we develop a carefully thought-out plan, versus plunging in and trying something new? The partnership with Lyft and the acquisition of Cruise Automation enable GM to take relatively low-risk, incremental steps toward autonomous driving, such as experimenting with semi-autonomous cars with Lyft drivers behind the wheel who can intervene if things go awry. GM leaders know that changes in insurance norms, liability law, customer acceptance, technology, and the competitive landscape will happen quickly. They know that they cannot plan everything, but if they jump in to begin learning, they will be prepared to adapt as events unfold.

Strategic Dilemma #4: When new capabilities are needed, should we build them internally, acquire, or partner? Lyft is expert at software and ride-sharing. Cruise Automation is expert at autonomous vehicle technology. GM knows manufacturing, and can quickly tap into long-established networks of suppliers to source tens of thousands of car parts. These complementary capabilities will allow GM to move much faster than if it pursued a go-it-alone strategy. GM probably sensed that if it acquired Lyft outright, it would kill the smaller company's ingenuity and entrepreneurial spirit. GM wisely invested enough to have a voice in Lyft's strategic decisions, but not so much that it squelched Lyft's culture and drove off its best talent. Similarly, GM will protect the three-year-old, 40-person culture of Cruise Automation by allowing it to operate as an independent unit within GM, based in Silicon Valley.

Strategic Dilemma #5: Can we afford to shed parts of our business in order to focus on future growth? Chief Executive Mary Barra has boldly cast off unprofitable parts of GM's business to allow greater focus on attractive growth opportunities, and to better prepare for an unpredictable future. In March 2017, the company announced the sale of its Opel business to Peugeot, which means GM is exiting the European market. The *Wall Street Journal* reported that Barra's move "produced considerable hand-wringing in the U.S.," where industry analysts and others accused GM of "short-sightedly abandoning a key global market."[7] The sale of Opel will make GM the only major automaker without a substantial presence in Europe. It will reduce GM's sales volume by 10 percent and knock the company out of the running to be the top global automaker. However, Barra's decision is not only courageous, but smart. Shedding Opel will free up money and management attention to invest in more-profitable markets (such as North America and China) and in future technologies, such as self-driving cars. The choice to shrink the business is a difficult one, but one that will undoubtedly better position GM for the future.

Although these five strategic dilemmas have existed since the beginning of time, they have become more acute and problematic in recent years for two key reasons: First, markets are changing faster, and companies in every sector have become more agile and faster moving. If you can't keep up, you get left behind. Take the example of the fashion industry. Until recent years, manufacturers traditionally introduced new products in two big clothing retail seasons, spring and fall.

This paradigm has been upended by fast-fashion retailers such as H&M, Zara, and Forever 21, which introduce a continuous stream of new products not tied to any particular season. Zara introduces 40,000 new products every year—shipping them to stores twice a week. It gets fast, continuous feedback on what's selling and what's not, then adjusts the next week's shipments based on minute-to-minute trends. Facing these fast-adapting competitors, formerly popular brands such as Aeropostale, American Apparel, and PacSun have fallen out of favor with shoppers, and have filed for bankruptcy protection. When markets are changing fast, it's crucial to learn constantly and adapt continuously to avoid obsolescence.

Second, the historical sources of competitive advantage, such as capital equipment, brand equity, and proprietary expertise and technology, are both less valuable and more perishable in today's fast-changing world. Why? Companies can outsource nearly any function, so new competitors can pop up quickly, seemingly out of nowhere. Patents, expertise, and knowledge are difficult to protect, and become outdated quickly. Consumers are less brand-loyal and their behaviors change fast. (Who would have imagined, five or 10 years ago, that in one-third of marriages, spouses would have met online?) Technology can be replicated easily. For all these reasons, we *need* to move faster and more fearlessly to capture new opportunities when they arise, or we may quickly become irrelevant.

In this climate, many of the strategic rules we formerly lived by have become obsolete. Rules such as "Stick to your knitting," "Plan, then do," "Ask your customers what they want," and "Release a major upgrade every year or two" didn't anticipate a time when flexibility and speed would be so crucial for success.

Should We Be Worried?

The history of business throughout the past couple of decades is replete with stories of companies that failed to move fast enough as their markets changed around them. Blockbuster failed to respond quickly enough to the disruptive presence of Netflix in the DVD rental, and then the video-streaming markets. Kodak was famously slow to adopt the technology it had itself invented—digital photography— until other companies had staked out unassailable claims to the market. BlackBerry Ltd. and Nokia failed to respond quickly enough as the Apple iPhone and other innovative smartphones left the companies in the dust.

These companies are not anomalies. The average lifespan of an S&P 500 company was 61 years in 1958, and is only 20 years today.[8] An S&P 500 company is replaced every two weeks.

On the other hand, companies that start from scratch, including the more than 100 "unicorn" startups (those with valuations of more than $1 billion), such as Uber, Snapchat, Airbnb, Palantir, and others, start out with none of established companies' advantages of size, assets, and employee base, yet they seem to have another advantage. Because these startups have little or nothing to lose if they fail, they can fearlessly innovate. And if a startup does fail, which many do, the founders, executives, and employees can simply either start up a new venture, or move on to another company.

Large, long-established companies, and the executives who run them, don't have that luxury. They have *plenty* to lose, both organizationally and personally, if they fail.

Despite the success of some of these start-from-scratch companies, it's my belief that the more exciting stories are being created today by giant, long-established companies—companies that have tremendous capacity to create new value for the world, provided they learn to grow fearlessly.

What Does Fearless Growth Look Like?

To be able to respond quickly and intelligently to the fast pace of change in the world, we need all levels and functions in our businesses to be creative and responsive. We need speed. Said Ginni Rometty—chairwoman, president, and CEO of IBM—in an interview with the *New York Times*, "People ask, 'Is there a silver bullet?' The silver bullet, you might say is speed, this idea of speed."[9]

Do you think your own business is quick enough and agile enough to survive and thrive in today's fast-moving business markets? One way to get some idea of whether or not that is the case is to take a simple diagnostic that will provide you with a yardstick for just how fast and fearless your business really is.

To what extent would you say each of the following are true about your business? (Give your company a "5" for each statement that is always or to a great extent true, a "3" for statements that are sometimes or partly true, and a "1" for statements that are false.)

- We are ambitious, setting out to do something truly new and groundbreaking that creates enormous new value for the world.
- We anticipate what is likely to change in our business environment, and the new opportunities that these changes may create.
- When we see an opportunity, we develop a smart and differentiated way of addressing it, and we take action immediately to begin to learn.
- We focus appropriate parts of our business on efficiency, consistency, and predictability, and other parts on exploration and innovation.
- We have the courage to displace our existing offerings with new solutions. We would rather disrupt ourselves than be disrupted by others, and would rather create the future than have it forced upon us.
- We don't restrict our strategic options to only those we can accomplish with our current capabilities. If new capabilities are required to reach our strategic goals, we build or acquire these over time.
- When something unexpected happens—a data breach, a new competitor, a new customer need—we communicate rapidly to make a decision, and take action quickly.

- When we make a strategic decision, we ask, "What action can we take tomorrow to put this in action, and to begin to learn?"
- We constantly experiment, finding low-risk, immediate ways to test strategic alternatives. What works, we keep. What doesn't, we fix or discard.
- We're attuned to the damper that incentives can put on growth. We have flexible budgeting and performance management systems. We hold people accountable, but also allow for changes in strategy.
- Our strategies are fluid and designed for learning. We continuously adjust and evolve our plans as we encounter new information, and when the business environment changes.

This list gives you a glimpse of what it feels like to be fast and fearless. If you gave your company 1s, 2s, or 3s on more than half of these statements, you are probably struggling to move as fast or as fearlessly as you would like. In that case, how can you get from where you are now to where you would like to be? Using the examples of highly successful companies that have grown fearlessly, this book is here to tell you how.

Barriers to Fearless Growth

Since the Industrial Revolution, consistency has been synonymous with business excellence. The quality and Six Sigma movements were built on the need to drive out variation in business processes. And indeed, consistency is still crucial in our businesses. We would rather fly on an airline that consistently departs (and arrives) on time, and we dine at McDonald's because their French fries taste exactly the same at every location worldwide.

However, the very things that created great success for many large companies are now leading to their declining performance. In today's fast-moving world, creativity is essential to staying relevant and vital, yet the drive for consistency and efficiency can squelch our ability to be creative, and to explore. It seems the more a company excels at exploiting its current assets and capabilities, the worse it performs at spotting and addressing new opportunities. The better it is at optimizing performance within its current business model, the worse it is at developing new business models.

Why is it so hard to grow fast and fearlessly? Despite the apparent advantages that large, established companies possess—the skilled workforces, the R&D centers and patents, the massive distribution networks, the knowledgeable salesforces, and installed base of customers—many of these companies are stalled, and have trouble achieving growth. The fact is: In many large businesses, there are an array of tenacious, hard-to-budge barriers and obstacles to growth.

In conversations with executives at a number of large, established companies, I have heard the following barriers to spotting emerging opportunities and acting on them quickly:

- **Risk.** "We have a lot to lose if things go wrong. We've invested for decades to build our brand equity, distribution channel, customer relationships, and people, and we hesitate to put any of these at risk to go after a new opportunity."
- **Investor expectations.** "Our investors expect consistency. Doing new things requires investment, and meeting quarterly earnings expectations always wins out over investing in new business directions that may take months—or years—to reach profitability."
- **No crisis.** "It's hard to change when we are doing well. There is no 'burning platform' forcing us to take action.

If there were a crisis—a dramatic drop in market share, or disappointing financial results—we might be motivated to move faster."

- **Capability gaps.** "Our skills and capabilities are oriented to running business as usual, not to trying new things."
- **Customer inertia.** "Our business-to-business customers are very conservative about trying new things. It takes them years to test and implement a new product. They can't change fast, so we can't change fast."
- **Incentives and policies.** "Our processes, policies, and performance incentives were created to minimize cost and risk, not to support innovation."
- **Employee capacity.** "Our employees at all levels are maxed out. We've continually asked them to do more with less. They're hunkered down, and are focusing on the essentials of running the business, not innovating for growth. Sticking your neck out to put forth a new idea might just land more work in your lap."
- **Identity.** "Our identity—the way we think of ourselves, the type of people we hire and promote—is linked to our historic strengths, not the capabilities we'll need in the future."

There is an almost endless number of reasons why big companies have trouble combining their size with speed and agility. These many different reasons can be distilled down into a handful of principles. In my book *The Agility Advantage* I revealed five primary obstacles to moving quickly and decisively in response to changes in their markets:

1. Companies lose touch with customers, and leaders lose touch with their own employees. As a result, they receive poor, late, or biased information—or no information at

all—about emerging customer needs, changes in competitor capabilities, or the possibilities new technologies are creating. When a new opportunity does arise, they often fail to see and act on it.

2. Companies employ financial incentives that motivate short-term thinking and doing "more of the same." To compound this, many leaders do not know how to deal with unpredictability in a systematic way. They therefore hesitate to take action without irrefutable data supporting the new direction.

3. Leaders become wrapped up in daily challenges and business as usual, which keeps them from investing time in imagining what the future might hold or how they might take advantage of coming changes. They fail to effectively bridge corporate silos and encourage real debate regarding their company's future direction.

4. Organizational structure gets in the way. I met with an executive at a leading supplier of financial services technologies. I knew that the company had identified a major new product opportunity more than five years ago, so I asked him how they were moving ahead. "We haven't made much progress," he explained. "The capabilities we need to pursue this are spread across three or four different business units. Each would get credit for only a small portion of the revenue, so they have little incentive to go after the opportunity."

5. Even if companies see opportunities and make a timely decision to pursue them, leaders often fail to communicate the compelling, inspiring vision required to harness their employees' full energy, creativity, and agility.

With the right capabilities and mindset, organizations can spot new opportunities, act quickly, and establish new sources of competitive advantage. This book focuses on the hard choices we must make to be successful in the new economy, and how we can surmount the most-common barriers to speed and growth.

What It Takes to Grow in Today's Fast-Changing World

Make no mistake about it: Growing fearlessly in today's fast-changing world may require a bold change in your company's culture and ways of doing business.

Fearless growth requires reaching out to customers, employees, vendors, and communities to gather their good ideas. It requires long-term thinking, and the willingness to let go of some of the things that formerly made you successful. It requires taking risks, taking action before you feel fully prepared, and learning from each failure and setback. It requires leaders to set aside time from day-to-day firefighting to imagine what the future might hold and to determine how best to capitalize on future changes. It requires a fluid organization that accelerates change rather than stopping change in its tracks. And it requires leaders to communicate a compelling and inspiring vision of the future.

Learning to grow fearlessly is like learning to ride a bike. When not in motion, the bike is tippy and unstable. As a child, when I was a first-time rider, getting on that wobbly bike was scary. Once I started moving fast, however, the bike was actually *more* stable. So it is with the new rules of fearless growth. Before you experience growing fearlessly, obeying the rules that I lay out in this book can be scary. After you become proficient, however, growing fearlessly feels—and is—safer and easier than staying put, doing the things you've always done. *You reach a point of dynamic stability, in which constant growth and adaptation create unstoppable success and resilience.*

The New Rules for Fearless Growth

This book is built on a foundation of seven powerful rules, each of which comes from my work with some of today's largest and most successful businesses. These businesses have proved that they are built to last, spotting trends and opportunities as they emerge, and then taking quick, effective action to achieve revenue growth.

Implementing these new rules can feel risky at first. To implement the rules, you have to give up some degree of control—to partners, customers, employees, and others. However, once you hit your stride, adhering to these rules *reduces* your risk. Because you have involved your customers in innovation, you will have greater insight into their changing needs and will be blindsided by customer defections less often. Because you will partner, borrow, and share, you will have more flexible capacity and capability—of assets, talent, data, knowledge, and ideas—to pursue revenue growth opportunities. Because you will have given more decision-making power to your employees, you will be more tuned in to changes in the marketplace, and will be able to respond more quickly when conditions change. You will have more creative thinkers and doers—partners, employees, customers, and others—to rely on, in a trusted way. You'll be faster at making decisions, and more resilient and adaptable in executing your strategies.

Implementing the new rules of fearless growth enables you to grow faster and in a less risky way. *Becoming proficient at changing and adapting makes you more stable, and giving up control enables you to gain control.*

In Table 1.1, I summarize the unspoken old rules of business, and compare them to the seven new rules that I lay out in future chapters. After the table, I provide a detailed description of each of the new rules.

Table 1.1:

The New Rules for Fearless Growth

Old Rules	New Rule	Implications
Strive for certainty and consistency. Avoid risk.	Rule #1: Embrace Uncertainty	View uncertainty in markets, technologies, and competitive landscape as an opportunity to build new competitive advantage. Be aware of bias. Manage risk effectively.
Do market research periodically to understand customer needs. Introduce major product upgrades every year or so.	Rule #2: Get in Sync With Customers	Gain continuous customer feedback. Get customers involved in developing, selling, and delivering your products. Update and improve products continuously. Enable customers to customize your offerings, and learn from the choices they make. Cater to and learn from outlier customers.
Own or take responsibility for every aspect of your value chain, from research and development, to operations, to sales and marketing. Avoid sharing data, technology, and knowledge. Rely on internal expertise as much as possible.	Rule #3: Partner, Borrow, and Share	Increase the flow of talent, data, assets, technology, and knowledge into and out of the company. This flow will leverage the ideas and capabilities outside your organization, while strengthening the people, processes, and capabilities inside your organization.

Conduct relationships with each customer, supplier, and channel partner independently.	Rule #4: Connect and Strengthen Your Ecosystem	Enhance the frequency and richness of interaction between your customers, suppliers, channel partners, content providers, and others. Host events, make introductions, and create technology platforms to connect ecosystem members.
Create hierarchical organizational structures that stay in place for years. Make decisions at the top. Provide employees with detailed instructions for how to do their jobs.	Rule #5: Open the Floodgates of Employee Creativity	Create cross-functional teams to attack particular opportunities, and grant them leeway to get the job done. Disband teams when their mission is complete. Enable employees to choose their own work. Connect employees across organizational silos. Establish fast feedback loops and clear values to guide employee activity.
Pursue only those growth opportunities that are achievable using your current capabilities.	Rule #6: Achieve Fast and Fearless Learning	Pursue attractive growth opportunities, even if they require your company to acquire substantially new capabilities. Set clear and aggressive learning goals. Make fast, focused learning a prime objective.

Allow trust to form naturally between employees and organizational units, and between your organization and your partners. Take action to create or restore trust only when trust is violated.	Rule #7: Build Trust Into All You Do	Recognize the immense impact of trust on efficiency and speed. Take deliberate action to build trust. Encourage and expect creative conflict, debate, and dissent.

Rule #1: Embrace Uncertainty

Nothing is certain in business, and every day brings new challenges and new opportunities. The only thing certain is that an overemphasis on predictability and an inability to understand and manage risk will kill a business. To grow fearlessly, you must learn to embrace and exploit uncertainty.

Companies that grow fearlessly know that highly predictable markets often create situations in which all competitors look more or less alike, and margins are thin. They know that market uncertainties can create new opportunities to differentiate, and to pull ahead of competitors. They are willing to take prudent risks, and know how to manage risk. They operate confidently amid uncertainty.

Rule #2: Get in Sync With Customers

Your customers are a remarkably powerful and often underutilized source of ideas for new products and services, improved current offerings, and new ways to do business. By closely collaborating with customers, paying attention to outliers, and observing how customers customize and use your products, you can be ready for whatever the future may bring.

Although they may make mistakes along the way, organizations that grow fearlessly have learned that it is critically important to get early versions of their products into customers' hands as quickly as they possibly can in order to gain early feedback and to avoid bringing the wrong product to market.

Within the most agile large companies, even top executives build customer interaction into their routines. They work in the field, observe the inner workings of their business, and regularly talk with employees, customers, and suppliers. Home Depot executives work in the stores, helping customers find products and providing advice, just as a typical store associate would. As a result, these leaders have a visceral view of their business, and a keen instinct for what is and what is not going to work. They spot market change as it is happening, and are ready to respond instantly and in a practical way.

Getting a head start does wonders for your speed. If you are running when you cross the starting line, you'll pass all of your competitors the moment the race begins.

Rule #3: Partner, Borrow, and Share

Up until a decade or so ago, companies needed large amounts of physical assets and many employees to become big. This is no longer the case. No longer do companies have to "do everything" to be successful. If you know what you want to accomplish, you can access the assets, talent, and capabilities of your people, and the world, to achieve your goals. Businesses that grow fearlessly crowdsource, outsource, and make use of freelancers, bloggers, microbusinesses, individual innovators, and myriad partners to achieve far more than they could on their own.

Companies don't need physical assets to grow huge in terms of reach and value. Alibaba is the most valuable company in Asia and the third most valuable retail brand in the world, but it has no inventory. Airbnb has a market capitalization greater than Marriott, but it owns no hotels or real estate. Uber is the world's largest car service, but it owns no cars.

Nor are a lot of employees always needed to pursue major growth opportunities. Cisco CEO John Chambers predicts: "Soon you'll see huge companies with just two employees—the CEO and the CIO."[10] Although this may be an exaggeration, his point is valid. Everything you need to become big in terms of revenues and value to the world can be accomplished without taking on a large number of employees, and the payroll, perks, facilities, and other overhead that come with them. Most functions, including R&D, manufacturing, customer service, sales, and marketing can all be outsourced, or even crowd-sourced, so that big, established companies can go after new growth opportunities without distracting or reconfiguring the core business.

Rule #4: Connect and Strengthen Your Ecosystem

Most companies that are big and growing fast today don't just sell products and services; they create, and profit from, entire ecosystems. Google, Facebook, Twitter, Airbnb, and other "new economy" businesses are prime examples of this trend. When you create the right ecosystem for your company, it will take on a life of its own and grow itself.

Airbnb didn't get big by acquiring assets. It grew larger, with more accommodations than any other hotelier, by coming up with an idea, and connecting a community to make that idea reality. Airbnb's founders were passionately committed to solving the problem of connecting individuals who had extra space in their homes with people who needed a place to stay and were up for a travel adventure. Before Airbnb, taking someone into your home for the night, or staying in someone's home, was risky business. You didn't know who to trust. Airbnb solved this problem by creating a platform for guests and hosts to score each other. Hosts who exaggerate or misrepresent their accommodations, and those who are dirty, unreliable, or discourteous are quickly brought back in line. And payment is safe and secure.

My most fastidious friend, a woman who finds fault with the cleanliness of many hotels, loves Airbnb. If the reviews say the accommodation is clean, she knows it will be clean. She enjoys making friends with her hosts and having access to advice about local haunts, great places to eat, and how to escape the tourist trail. With relatively few employees, Airbnb created an ecosystem of guests and hosts to make all of this happen.

Building an ecosystem entails risk. You cannot always control who will join and how members will interact with each other. However, once an ecosystem gets going, it becomes self-sustaining. It enables fearless growth.

Rule #5: Open the Floodgates of Employee Creativity

Employees are seldom inspired by leaders who implore them to grow revenues or increase share price. These measures feed executive bonuses, but don't fuel the motivation or creativity of the people who can make or break your business: the employees who are designing your next new product, the financial analysts who are devising a breakthrough way to help managers visualize their business, the customer service representatives who jump through hoops to expedite an important customer's shipment, and the sales and service employees who are face to face with customers every day.

Employees want to be engaged in their work, and want to contribute to something greater than themselves. Too often, however, we squander their talent by over-measuring, micromanaging, and failing to inspire. We fail to facilitate employees' natural desire to collaborate with others and to grow their own skills. Give employees the power, knowledge, and network they need, and you will unlock vast power.

To thrive amid rapid changes in culture, technology, and competition, leaders must instill a passionate desire in the hearts of all employees. Employees must intimately understand what they are collectively trying to achieve, for whom, and why. For example, Google's corporate purpose is clear and inspiring: "Organizing the world's information and making it universally accessible and useful." This purpose leaves plenty of room for trying new things, and it encourages big thinking. The company sets out to develop solutions that are 10 times better than what currently exists.

Having a big ambition by aiming to do something truly new and groundbreaking is a first step, but merely having a grand vision is not enough. Vision needs to be accompanied by an impatience to take action. Instead of waiting on the sidelines, organizations must be biased toward taking action immediately, and sustaining this action despite the inevitable roadblocks and setbacks.

This transition from vision to action is where many companies fail. They take too long to make decisions, intent on eliminating every risk before proceeding. Or they punish employees who get too far ahead of company management, instead of rewarding them for their initiative. Or their organizations are slow to move, clogged with layer after layer of bureaucracy that derails projects and the people who champion them instead of speeding them on their way. Companies that grow fearlessly ensure that all their employees understand the vision, and they empower employees to take bold action in support of the vision.

Rule #6: Achieve Fast and Fearless Learning

When Facebook went public in 2012, investors and industry analysts were skeptical of the company's ability to make the shift from online advertising to mobile advertising. Consumers were shifting in mass numbers to using mobile, and many young people used only mobile. Meanwhile, Facebook had zero revenue in mobile advertising.

Throughout the next four years, the company started to dominate mobile advertising. Facebook generates 30 percent of total mobile ad revenue, and mobile ad revenue makes up 80 percent of the company's total ad revenue.

The strategy fueling Facebook's impressive revenue growth is constant, massive-scale experimentation. Facebook runs hundreds of different versions of its site at any given time. The company measures customer response, then retains the versions that perform the best and eliminates the poorer-performing versions. In time, this improves the experience for users and improves results for advertisers.

Although your business may not learn as fast as Facebook does, this "experimentation mindset" is crucial to maintaining relevance in today's fast-changing world. For example, UPS knows that regulations may someday require lower emissions and fuel efficiency, so it has a "rolling laboratory" of 11 different types of alternative-fuel and advanced technology vehicles in use today. Some work best in dense urban areas, where stopping every few blocks to deliver a package is necessary. Others work best in rural areas, where it might be 300 miles between stops. UPS is ahead of regulations in learning how to optimize each vehicle for these different conditions.

Fast learning is the most valuable competitive advantage a company can build. Keenly observing the business environment, taking action before you feel fully ready, and incorporating what you've learned immediately into your strategy are tickets to playing in today's fast-changing global economy. An organization that learns continuously can achieve stability and safety even while in motion, just like riding a bike.

Rule #7: Build Trust Into All You Do

Business is built on a foundation of relationships with employees, business partners, customers, and those in the communities in which we work. Trust is the ingredient that enables the establishment and growth of these relationships, and allows us to respond quickly without worrying whether or not our key stakeholders will be fully engaged and supportive of our initiatives. When we trust that our colleagues will do their part, we can set more aggressive goals, place bigger bets, and have a bigger imagination about what may be possible.

When we trust our coworkers, we feel comfortable engaging in the debate and disagreement required to make sound decisions. When we trust our business partners, we can move faster together, navigating the uncertain terrain with the confidence that we will each treat each other fairly when we encounter unexpected failures or successes. When we abandon the old rules and shift to the new, we create the ability to grow fearlessly.

In Conclusion

Being big, fast, and fearless isn't easy, but it *can* and *is* being done by some of today's most successful large businesses. In the chapters that follow, I provide compelling examples of companies that are making it work. As you read through these chapters, put yourself in the shoes of the men and women who run these companies. How do the new rules apply to *your* business? How can you adapt them to your company's unique processes and culture? How can you leverage them to the benefit of your customers, your vendors and suppliers, your people, your investors, and the communities in which you do business?

Answer these questions, and your company will be poised for fearless growth.

Rule #1: Embrace Uncertainty

On June 23, 2016, the citizens of the United Kingdom voted to leave the European Union, and the stability that the UK had enjoyed for decades as a result of its EU membership was replaced with massive uncertainty overnight. Most surveys conducted in the days leading up to the vote showed that the majority of voters expected that "remain" would win. Financial markets and bets placed with bookies also strongly favored "remain" winning.

The surveys, betting shops, and financial markets were all wrong.

The day after the "Brexit" (*British exit*) vote, UK financial markets went wild. The pound fell to a 31-year low against the dollar, and the FTSE 250 slumped 7 percent (it has since recovered to pre-vote levels). UK government bonds set record lows in the aftermath of the vote, and Standard & Poor cut the UK's sterling AAA credit rating—the top rating category—two levels, to AA. S&P cited Brexit as the reason for the downgrade, explaining that the vote would "weaken the predictability, stability, and effectiveness of policy-making in the UK."[1]

Companies in every industry—from airlines, to energy, to telecom—were worried about the effects of the UK's decision to leave the European Union, and many made moves to downsize, citing uncertainty that they faced in their operations and markets. Lloyds Banking Group announced that it would cut 3,000 jobs; French business-class airline La Compagnie cut capacity, making plans to halt flights between London and New York City; Mondelez International even shrunk the size of the UK version of its Toblerone chocolate bars, citing higher costs.

Natural Fear of Uncertainty Is the Biggest Barrier to Speed

From humanity's earliest days on this planet, people have tried to make the uncertain world more certain and more predictable. They have attempted to determine when game animals would be plentiful and when they would be sparse, when to plant and harvest their crops to avoid seasonal damage and maximize yields. Throughout human history, people have built cities, businesses, governments, and infrastructures to bring predictability and certainty to their lives.

Why do we tend to flee from uncertainty and seek certainty? According to psychologists, we humans are hardwired to dislike uncertainty; it's in our DNA. In a recent study, researchers discovered that uncertainty is more stressful to humans than knowing that something bad is definitely going to happen. This mechanism is controlled by the *striatum*—a structure buried deep within our brains that is commonly known as the "reward center." This reward center directly affects our decision-making, motivation, and perceptions of risk and reward. In addition to anticipating both good and bad consequences—and pushing us toward good ones while steering us away from bad ones—the striatum can assess (though often inaccurately) the odds of these consequences actually occurring.

It is therefore no surprise that business leaders naturally tend to prefer certainty over uncertainty. As McKinsey authors John Dowdy and Kirk Rieckhoff summarized, "Individuals worry about being wrong, making a superior angry, or alienating other parts of the organization." They continue, "Individuals rationally seek ever more information, conduct additional analysis, build consensus, await direction or permission, or optimize for those most important to them (their 'tribe'), rather than the enterprise. This often results in lowest-common-denominator recommendations to senior leaders."[2]

To compound this, we reward leaders for bringing certainty to their businesses. We reward them with bonuses and promotions for meeting revenue and profit targets set many months in advance. We thank them for keeping surprises to a minimum.

Regardless of what industry they're in, companies have worked to minimize the effects of uncertainty on their operations, and on their bottom lines. They've invested in achieving consistency, efficiency, and scale. And although the need to continually enhance efficiency and predictability will never go away, too much focus on these things can make businesses less agile and less able to respond quickly to changes in their business environment.

In fact, failure to embrace and manage uncertainty is one of the biggest barriers I have witnessed to business speed. To overcome this barrier, perhaps we need to embrace the element of risk that speed can bring. Denise Mueller, a 43-year-old mother of three, and the world's fastest woman, explains why riding a bike at more than 140 miles per hour quiets her mind and brings peace. "You can't focus on anything but what's right in front of you. . . . When I get in that zone, it's like nirvana, that sense of focus when it all comes down to life or death."[3]

Wouldn't it be nice if we, as companies, could get "in the zone," where speed and even business risk only heighten our focus, clarity, and effectiveness?

How Uncertain Market Conditions Create Opportunity

Most everything in business is subject to change, often when you least expect it. And change brings uncertainty, which often manifests as fear, doubt, or paralysis. We don't know what's going to happen, so we wait. Most leaders consider uncertainty to be a negative, and do everything in their power to bring certainty and stability into their organizations and markets.

But what if, instead of being a negative, uncertainty in business was a positive? In my experience, this is often the case. Why? Because uncertainty creates opportunities to pull ahead of the competition and stay ahead. And businesses that are willing to take on more risk and operate in uncertain environments can win a competitive advantage over those that are not.

Indeed, whereas the Brexit vote negatively affected many businesses, others benefited in its wake. Premier Oil expects to save $100 million on its Catcher Field North Sea project, and GlaxoSmithKline plans to invest $360 million to increase capacity at three UK plants due to higher sales and profits.

Certainly, then, a willingness to operate in uncertain environments can be a competitive advantage. Therefore, we need to be sure that decision-makers in our companies have the right risk mentality and are willing to take on prudent risk. Billy Medof is president of Georgia-Pacific Corrugated Packaging—a unit of Koch Industries. In a presentation to one of Setili & Associates' 2016 Strategic Agility Think Tank events, Medof explained the importance of understanding risk and educating the leaders in your business about what level of risk they should be taking.

Shareholders often have higher risk tolerance than individual managers, who might think about risk quite conservatively. As a business unit leader, I might look at a P&L loss for the year as being catastrophic—my bonus and that of my team will be affected, as would our self-worth and our perception of how we might progress career-wise. My shareholder, on the other hand, has a greater appetite for risk. He may have 50 projects or businesses in his portfolio, so his risk on my particular business is balanced with that of other businesses. Shareholders always don't want us to forgo taking a hard swing at the ball just to have a less-risky and mediocre, but positive result.[4]

Clearly, uncertainty can have a tremendous effect on the fortunes of businesses and the men and women who run them. However, in my experience, companies benefit from embracing uncertainty rather than from avoiding it. It's what makes organizations like Kabbage, Koch Industries, Tesla, and the Walt Disney Studios big winners in a very uncertain world.

The following ideas are ways in which fast and unpredictable changes in your business environment can create a competitive advantage, despite the uncertainty.

Marketplace changes create new opportunities for us to surge ahead of competitors. When the world is certain, even mediocre companies can perform adequately. The world plods along much as it always has. Companies serve known customers, providing for well-understood, long-standing needs. The trouble is, in highly certain times, when nothing much is changing, companies tend to become more and more alike. In search of growth, they go after one another's customers, or drop price to gain market share. Margins get squeezed. It's okay for everyone, but great for no one.

Uncertain business environments, on the other hand, create the potential for companies to break out of the pack. When something unexpected happens—a new technology, a new competitor, a new customer need, or a change in governmental policy or regulations—it gives alert and prepared companies a chance to speed ahead if they respond in a faster, smarter, and more adaptive way to make the most of the new situation.

The faster and more surprising the change, the greater the advantage for companies that respond quickly. Company leaders who welcome marketplace changes and think, "How can I exploit this, before my competitors do?" rather than "Let's hunker down to watch, and hope this goes away," are able to take fast action, and can make the best of even difficult situations. Managing *well* in uncertain environments, to minimize risk while taking advantage of changes that occur in the business environment, is an uncommon capability that can be a tremendous source of competitive advantage.

A business unit president I work with was concerned when she noticed that sales in the Midwest region had plummeted in the space of just two months. After a series of conference calls with salespeople in the region, we discovered the reason: A competitor had begun offering same-day delivery and directly targeting all of my client's best customers. We acted fast, identifying a set of products that my client could reliably deliver in a two-hour time frame, using company-owned delivery vehicles. The competitor, who was using third-party logistics firms for delivery, couldn't match this offer, and sales rebounded, surpassing even their former level.

We can take simple steps to be more prepared for the unexpected. Anticipating a wide range of possible future scenarios, and having a frank discussion with other leaders in your firm about what you should do to prepare for the possibilities, is essential to preparing for the unexpected. Of course, we can't predict the future, but through this type of discussion, it often dawns on us that there are a few "no-brainer" steps we can take to be ready for what might happen. For example, fast-food restaurants that specialize in chicken likely have a plan for how to respond quickly with substitute sources of protein if a fast-spreading virus decimates chicken supplies.

Scenario-planning exercises can help us to become more deliberate in watching for the early warning signals of future market disruption. As part of their strategic planning process, leaders at PSCU, the leading credit union service organization, assessed current trends, and then identified a number of potential future scenarios. The scenarios differed in terms of competitor activity, technology evolution, consumer behavior, and other factors. This exercise enabled PSCU leaders to anticipate how they might adjust the company's strategy, depending on how the business environment changes over time. Company leaders identified a set of market signals and metrics to watch closely that would provide an early indication of which potential scenario was most likely to occur. For example, market signals might include things such as the degree of consumer adoption of payment alternatives such as Apple Pay and Android Pay. Keeping a careful eye on these market signals will enable PSCU to adapt its strategy very quickly when changes in its markets occur. Brandi Quinn, senior vice president of enterprise reporting and corporate secretary, explains:

> PSCU is a cooperative, so we are continually scanning the horizon for opportunities and threats that the credit unions we serve need to be aware of and prepared for. The financial services industry is changing incredibly fast, as a result of new financial technologies and emerging players, and consumers have many choices for payments and lending relationships. Just like any company, we have limited resources and

need to choose wisely about which new technologies to invest in, and when. We watch key market signals and metrics, so we have early warning if there is a need to shift gears or change direction.[5]

The more we proactively change the business environment, the greater control we have over business outcomes and competitive advantage. Martial arts experts know that if you want to be faster than someone with fast reactions, you have to create the situation. Consider how you can shape your business environment to preempt an effective competitive response.

One company I know was superb at helping to shape future regulations and industry technical standards—to its own advantage. Another was adept at developing new distribution channels that the competition hadn't considered, and would have a hard time penetrating quickly. Both companies kept their strategies under wraps during several months of negotiation and preparation with other parties. As a result, other players were caught by surprise, and were slow and relatively ineffective at responding.

We can create new profit streams by reducing the risk and uncertainty for our customers, especially in volatile markets. If your company is good at spotting the opportunities inherent to uncertain business environments, and at managing amidst uncertainty, consider how you can create new sources of growth and profit by reducing the risk of your customers, or even your suppliers. Insurance companies are masters at this, but every company should keep their eyes open for opportunities to do so.

A tire company I know reduced uncertainty for its suppliers by committing to "take or pay" for certain volumes of raw materials each month. In return for this concession, suppliers gave the company lower prices. Even more important, however, was the fact that by reducing supplier risk, the tire company ensured that suppliers would be economically healthy and able to ramp up supplies quickly when the market demanded it. Removing risk for suppliers created a greater ability for the tire company to thrive in an uncertain market.

Customer and market data, combined with artificial intelligence, can dramatically increase our ability to make fast decisions amid risk and uncertainty. Artificial intelligence and data are driving innovations across agriculture, automotive, energy, retail, weather, sports, and nearly every other arena. In many cases, these innovations have transformed the customer experience and brought tremendous new efficiency and value. These innovations also have the potential to reduce risk while increasing speed.

Kabbage specializes in making loans of up to $100,000 to small businesses. The small business market is inherently risky: Only about half of small businesses survive their first five years. Small businesses that fail often default on their loans in the process. Kabbage spotted this uncertainty and decided to exploit it. The company built a system to allow small businesses to qualify for loans and receive the funds in *minutes*—if the companies give Kabbage access to online data that provides a window into the health of their business, and their capacity to repay the loan. This includes UPS data on shipments, eBay and Amazon order data, and even social media data. If the loan applicant has a healthy stream of orders coming in, Kabbage is happy to provide a loan. Kabbage solved a big problem in small business lending by *reducing* risk and uncertainty, and providing small business with extremely fast access to funding. The company was rewarded for its efforts with a valuation of $1 billion dollars in late 2015.

Common Mistakes When Making Decisions in Uncertain Environments

Psychologists Daniel Kahneman and Amos Tversky, profiled in Michael Lewis's book *The Undoing Project*[6], were pioneers in discovering and describing the systematic decision-making mistakes people make under risk and uncertainty. At the time of their research, the prevailing economic theory assumed that people make logical, rational decisions. Though economists were slow to accept Kahneman and Tversky's conclusions, the conclusions are now widely accepted, and behavioral economists have expanded on the initial research. They have found that when we are aware of our own biases, we can reduce and counteract their effects.

The following ideas are biases I have observed slowing down companies in uncertain environments.

We see the facts that confirm what we think to be true, and tend to ignore other facts. Even very smart people who pride themselves on using "just the facts" to make decisions fall prey to *confirmation bias*—the tendency to see and remember information that confirms their preexisting beliefs or hypotheses. People tend to interpret ambiguous evidence as supporting their beliefs, subconsciously ignore or forget contradictory evidence, and selectively forget evidence that refutes their beliefs.

Confirmation bias is especially dangerous in fast-changing markets, because our beliefs about what will happen in the future are shaped mainly by what we've experienced in the past. Senior leaders of a manufacturing company that I once worked with believed strongly that its business-to-business customers would continue to favor domestic suppliers. "It's the relationship," they said. "Customers value the fact that our technical support reps can be there within two hours when they call. They can't afford to leave us for an offshore supplier." Despite the evidence—the rising availability of less expensive imported product, the cancellation of important contracts, and the presence of overseas suppliers at trade shows—the company continued to believe it was "safe" from imports, until it was too late.

Here are some things you can do to mitigate the impact of confirmation bias:

- Insist on disagreement and debate. Assign a team to "disprove" the predominant theory or to refute the most popular views on what will happen next in your markets.
- Bring in consultants, advisors, and other outsiders who you can count on to tell you the truth, rather than falling in line with the internal prevailing wisdom.
- When you encounter unexpected data, market information, or anecdotes from the field, identify three potential causes. This prevents jumping to a single conclusion, yet does not create so many potential causes that you don't have time to thoroughly investigate each one to find the true cause.
- Try other people's beliefs on for size.
- Communicate to others, and believe in your own mind, that you are ready to accept that your "truths" and beliefs may be wrong.
- Question authority.

We are willing to gamble on a large loss to avoid a small (but certain) loss. When all options are bad, we tend to place rash bets. I've seen this time and again when companies are faced with declining sales growth. Every option they see has significant downsides, so they embark on a highly risky strategy, such as acquiring another company that is also doing poorly, or acquiring a company that will be difficult to successfully integrate with their current business. They see no way out and figure, "Things can't get much worse so I may as well take a chance and hope to get lucky."

When you are in an uncertain market, the best strategic choice, rather than rushing into a desperate and ill-advised move, is often to accept the small but certain loss in the short run, and make plans to improve your competitive position to take advantage of future changes in the market.

We tend to choose a small but certain gain over a higher, but less certain gain. When choosing among attractive strategic options, in which a gain is expected, people often choose the safe bet. They would rather have a sure shot at growing 5 percent than a 70-percent chance of growing 15 percent (which has a higher "expected" value). However, placing only safe bets limits our upside potential.

The problem for so many companies—especially those that are publicly held—is that their leaders feel tremendous pressure to ensure certainty. They develop multiyear strategic plans and then feel committed to stick with the numbers they projected months or even years before. This focus on certainty and predictability limits their ability to exceed expectations. Why?

I've observed that company leaders who are very focused on achieving a certain revenue or profit number often fail to take advantage of opportunities to surpass the number. Let's say you're trying to grow your business unit's sales by 20 percent. Once you commit to your peers or boss that you are going to achieve that number, chances are you're not going to want to pursue a new opportunity that may allow you to double the size of your business. Doing so would put in jeopardy the 20-percent target that you already said you would achieve, so why take the risk—why put your own compensation or career in jeopardy? As a result of this thinking, you may forgo opportunities that could turn out to be successful ones for your business.

Companies that make a habit of shooting for the higher goal, while assiduously managing their initiatives to maximize their chances of success, prevail in the long run.

We errantly draw conclusions from small amounts of information. When assessing the attractiveness of alternative courses of action, it's often difficult or expensive to get as much data as we would like. This is especially true in fast-changing and unpredictable markets. We don't have the luxury of time, and very different conditions may exist in one part of the market versus the other. We ask five customers what they think, and hope that their views are representative of a larger group of customers. We talk to a handful of operations supervisors in our own organization to gain a view on whether or not our plan can be successfully implemented. We attempt to draw conclusions from the data we have, make a quick decision, and take action.

My research and expertise focuses on how companies can become faster in responding to market change, so there's no one who appreciates fast action more than I do. However, when we are relying on small, hastily gathered data sets to make decisions, it's crucial that we recognize the limitations of our knowledge. We can't learn from five customers what is likely to work with 5,000 customers. As long as we recognize the limitations of our small data set, we can establish a strategy that enables us to "learn as we go."

We pour good money after bad, to avoid selling at a loss. I've seen many companies continue to allow a weakly performing business unit to drag down profits, damage morale, and suck up inordinate management attention, all because company leaders do not want to sell it at a loss or admit defeat. Shutting down or divesting business units that do not fit with your strategy is critical for maintaining speed and focus.

We rely too much on superiors to make decisions. In *The Undoing Project*, author Michael Lewis tells a story about Delta Air Lines that illustrates this point. In the 1980s, Delta had a string of embarrassing mishaps, including pilots landing at the wrong airports. The head of training, Jack Maher, asked psychologist Amos Tversky for advice. "Captains at the time would be complete autocratic jerks who insisted on running the show," said Maher.[7] Tversky pointed out that the way to keep captains from making mistakes was to train others in the cockpit to question the captain's judgment. Once Delta changed the culture in the cockpit, the mistakes disappeared.

Types of Uncertainty

There are two primary types of uncertainty, and it is the interaction between these two that determines the amount of uncertainty you will face in your business and industry.

1. Demand uncertainty: How many customers will buy our product, how often, and at what price?
2. Delivery uncertainty: Can we develop and reliably deliver the offering that customers want? This uncertainty includes technical capability, service capability, and capacity.

The most uncertain businesses and industries are those that have both the greatest demand and delivery uncertainty, while the least uncertain businesses and industries are those with the lowest levels of both demand and delivery uncertainty.

It would be hard to imagine a business that has to deal with more uncertainty than Virgin Galactic—what founder Sir Richard Branson calls the world's first commercial space line.

First, there are the technological challenges of developing and building spacecraft from scratch that can be air launched, fly through suborbital space, and then land safely and reliably back on Earth. Indeed, in October 2014, a Virgin Galactic SpaceShipTwo vehicle—which is designed to carry a crew of two and six passengers—crashed in the Mojave Desert during flight testing, killing one of the pilots and seriously injuring the other. Not only did this event cast a dark shadow over the safety of Virgin Galactic's commercial space program, but it destroyed the only test aircraft the company had at the time—significantly delaying Richard Branson's plans to send tourists into space beginning in 2015.

Second, Virgin Galactic has also faced a tremendous number of regulatory challenges. The FAA was criticized for applying the same level of regulatory control over the newly birthed space tourism industry as it does to the fully mature airline industry—stifling growth and innovation. However, after the SpaceShipTwo crash, the FAA was criticized for relaxing or waiving some of those regulations. This kind of regulatory uncertainty makes business decisions more difficult, financing harder to obtain, and success less certain.

Then there are the customers. Are there enough people willing and able to pay the $250,000 fully paid-up deposits to make Virgin Galactic a going concern? The answer is apparently yes, at least in the near term. According to Virgin Galactic's website, about 700 people—between the ages of 10 to over 90, from more than 50 different countries—have paid their deposits and are anxiously awaiting the opportunity to become astronauts.[8] But once this initial rush of customers works its way through the queue, will Virgin Galactic's business model be sustainable? There are only so many people who can afford to pay such a high tariff to make a visit to space, even if the costs are reduced over time and the price is cut in half to "just" $125,000.

Regardless of all this uncertainty, there is an opportunity to profit when success does eventually come to the commercial space tourism industry—and Richard Branson is not alone in this belief. At least four other companies have jumped into the arena, including Blue Origin (founded by Amazon CEO Jeff Bezos), XCOR Aerospace (which reports that it has more than 350 passengers signed on), SpaceX, and World View.[9]

So, why should we embrace uncertainty when it seems that so many businesses have been built on a firm foundation of certainty, and we ourselves as humans are genetically wired to prefer it? The simple answer is because the world today is changing quickly; companies that are agile, fast, and adaptable in the face of uncertainty have an advantage over companies that are not. They seize opportunities that others avoid, and leverage them to their own benefit and to the benefit of customers and investors.

Not only that, but it is the companies—and the men and women who run them—that are willing to operate in uncertain conditions that move us forward as a society. Said venture capitalist Luke Johnson after the crash of Virgin Galactic's SpaceShipTwo, "These bold experiments lead to new inventions, new jobs, fresh choices for consumers, and overall a more prosperous world. Progress happens by trial and error—now and then these errors are painful and expensive, as with Virgin Galactic."[10]

On the other hand, what if you're operating in a stable market in which things are highly certain and unchanging? What then? Perhaps it's a good idea to introduce some uncertainty into it. The great industry disruptors of today have done just that: taking stable markets, upending them, and gaining massive market share and valuations as a result. Uber disrupted the highly regulated taxi industry, which hadn't changed much in the past 100 years, and today its valuation is $68 billion. Airbnb provided millions of people around the world an alternative to expensive hotels and resorts, short-circuiting the lodging industry and its traditional pricing models. Airbnb's value today? $30 billion. Netflix's streaming movie platform made brick-and-mortar video-rental stores like Blockbuster (which had 60,000 employees and more than 8,000 stores at its peak) obsolete. The result? Netflix thrived (with a current market cap of more than $67 billion) while Blockbuster went bankrupt.

Learn From the Film Industry

When you're willing to do business in an environment that is uncertain—one that keeps most other companies away—this gives you a competitive advantage. Consider the film industry. For every hit film that a major film studio has, bringing in hundreds of millions (or sometimes even billions) of dollars, it typically has many more failures. So why do so many people keep making films when so many films are doomed to fail? Because the upside can be tremendous. Global box office revenue for all films is anticipated to increase from a little more than $38 billion in 2016 to almost $50 billion in 2020.[11] On November 2, 2016, Walt Disney Studios proudly announced that it had its biggest year ever with $5.8 billion in global box office revenue through November 1st, with three films (*Captain America: Civil War, Zootopia*, and *Finding Dory*) each breaking the $1 billion mark in 2016 box office revenue.

Despite the uncertainty that is an inherent part of the film industry (and, in fact, a part of most creative industries, including music, performing, and visual arts, film, television, and publishing), many are willing to work within it, hoping to make a profit. So, what do filmmakers like Walt Disney Studios do to mitigate the uncertainty and risk in their industry?

Here are five strategies they follow to gain a competitive advantage over the competition:

1. **They place multiple bets.** Disney released 11 films in 2016. And although the company hoped they all would be blockbusters, Disney would still succeed if only a few reached blockbuster status. Consider how you can reduce your risk by trying more than one approach to solving any problem you face.

2. **They replicate their success to reduce risk.** Most film studios know the power of a good sequel, and Disney is no exception. Sequels have a built-in audience of people who liked the original version of the film, and who will want to see the next iteration. Many of the films on Disney's 2017 release schedule are sequels, including *Star Wars: Episode VIII, Toy Story 4*, and *Pirates of the Caribbean: Dead Men Tell No Tales*. Although doing "more of the same" has risks of its own, companies often fail to mine their own organizations for success stories that can be replicated.

3. **They right-size the budget.** Film studios keep budgets low for niche films, and pull out all the stops for the ones most likely to attract a large audience. Similarly, I've observed that successful companies right-size the budget for new ventures. One company I know granted $100,000 to a team that was excited about a new product so they could develop a proof of concept. The catch was that they had to entice a customer to also contribute $100,000 to the experiment. Since both sides had skin in the game, both worked hard to make the concept a success. Once they saw this success, the senior leadership team earmarked $700,000 more for the next phase of development. Right-sizing the investment to each step of the development process ensured that teams had the frugal mentality of an entrepreneur/business owner, while not hamstringing them due to lack of funds.

4. **They take what works in one medium, and apply it to another.** Already-existing franchises such as the Marvel comics characters and the wildly popular Harry Potter books are relatively safe bets for film studios. The studios not only build on successful comics and novels, they build on their films by offering toys, theme parks, and the like.

5. **They serve specific niches.** By serving a specific niche—teen, women, gay, and so on—filmmakers can ensure that they will have at least some audience interest in their film upon release. And if it crosses over to a broader audience, so much the better.

Managing Risk in Uncertain Environments

A few years ago, my husband, Rob, and I became kiteboarding enthusiasts. For those of you not familiar with kiteboarding (also known as kitesurfing), it's a sport in which you ride a wakeboard-style board, pulled along by a large kite 60 feet in the air. We have long been avid sailors, so the idea of riding through the waves while completing jumps and spins in the air using a kite was very appealing to us.

Kiteboarding is an incredibly fun thing to do, but it also has its dangers, just like any other sport.

One thing we do to mitigate the risks that go along with kiteboarding is to always have a buddy—someone who's there to help if things go wrong. Thunderstorms are common in the Southeast, so we both make a point of keeping an eye out for them. We even have special hand signals to communicate with each other when we're too far apart to talk.

We do the same thing in business. In a company, your buddy system can be your management team and employees. You collectively keep an eye out for things that could go wrong—a competitor that you are concerned about, a new technology that changes customer buying behavior, or a change in workforce availability. When everyone is vigilant and alert, you are more likely to spot threats coming and avert them successfully.

Rob and I consider a variety of factors and do a form of scenario analysis before we go out on the water, talking about potential strategies *before* unfolding events demand urgent action. In this way, we can mentally rehearse our potential response to future events. For example, what if a kite tears and becomes useless when we're far from shore and sunset is approaching? What would we do? What if the wind direction shifts and it becomes difficult to make it back to our starting point on shore? By considering all the things that might go wrong, and thinking through how we will deal with them, the risk is minimized. Similarly, businesses should anticipate and plan for things that may go wrong.

One highly effective company I know is particularly effective at managing the risks of each new project it undertakes. Company leaders identify the assumptions required to make the project successful, assumptions related to sales, product development, technology, partners, and so forth. They then assign a specific person in the company to manage each assumption. For example, an assumption may be that a new product can achieve a certain performance target, by a certain date. The person who owns this assumption is dedicated to assuring that this goal is met. They work with vendors to troubleshoot problems. They make sure the production process is designed to produce the product as specified, and line up trials at customer sites. By managing assumptions diligently, the company minimizes risk, and maximizes the chance that goals will be achieved.

In my book *The Agility Advantage*, I outline seven ways to manage risks in an uncertain business environment:

1. **Design your strategy to maximize learning.** When moving into risky strategic territory, think about what initial steps would enable you to understand what you need to learn to succeed. Then design your strategy to meet these learning objectives.

2. **Manage technology risk.** Ask yourself what objectives you could potentially achieve through technology advancement. What risks do these new technologies present? What development and learning will be required to employ them?

3. **Manage customer-demand risk.** Identify and set out to directly address consumer concerns that might stop customers from buying.

4. **Think from the ground up to develop a differentiated offering.** Ask yourself in what arenas your thinking has become constrained by established practices, beliefs, and norms. If you were to reduce your problem to its fundamental truths, what new and different solutions might your company produce?

5. **Be the best at something.** Define the target customer group your product or service will be ideally suited for, and the ways this group will regard yours as the very best available solution.

6. **Employ scenario analysis.** Discuss and debate potential scenarios and strategies for succeeding in them *before* such events demand urgent action. Teams that have talked frankly about the scenarios that might unfold can interpret events more rationally when they *do* occur.

7. **Recognize, manage, and test the assumptions required to succeed.** Understand clearly what assumptions must hold true for you to be successful with any strategic initiative, and take deliberate steps to manage these assumptions.[12]

The Need for Efficiency Clashes With the Need to Be Agile and Adaptable

In the past, companies and their systems and processes were built for consistency, efficiency, scale, and to mitigate risk. We have built our systems to drive out variation, to do it the same every time. This is still important. When we check into a hotel, we are comforted if the room looks, smells, and feels the same as others we have slept in of the same chain. We still want our packages to be delivered on time— even more so now that companies such as Amazon have built their reputation on fast, reliable delivery.

I define *agility* as the ability to identify new opportunities and capitalize on them quickly. Today, our businesses that were built for efficiency must now also be agile, with the ability to move quickly in the face of fast-changing market conditions.

However, efficiency and agility are at odds with each other. To be efficient, we need to have the attributes of a rowing team, which include precise timing and coordination, working as a well-oiled team, going in a straight line, creating minimal disruption to the water, and doing the same thing perfectly, over and over. A rowing shell is sleek and efficient.

To be agile, however, we need the attributes of a whitewater kayak, which include being maneuverable and adapting to new conditions continuously. A whitewater kayak can navigate well through turbulence, and sometimes it even benefits from turbulence.

The tension between being efficient like a rowing shell, and adaptable like a whitewater kayak, is a conundrum that many large companies find hard to resolve.

Perhaps no other company exemplifies efficiency better than Walmart. For decades, everything Walmart did was focused on driving costs out and improving consistency. For example, clothing sizes are consistent across every brand and manufacturer in the store, so when a customer carries an armful of garments to the dressing room, she can be sure that every piece fits the same.

Now, however, Walmart has found that adaptability is crucial. CEO Doug McMillon says, "Once upon a time a company like ours might have made big, strategic choices on an annual or quarterly cycle. Today strategy is daily. . . . As a CEO, you need to have a framework in your mind, but strategic thinking is much more fluid."[13]

Achieving Efficiency *and* Agility Within the Same Company

Organizational agility comprises both efficiency, which is the ability to quickly accomplish known objectives at the lowest cost and effort, and agility, which is the ability to learn and adjust course as conditions change. For example, adapt your strategy to changes in the market, new information and learning, and internal and external customer feedback.

Fortunately, there are ways to achieve *both* efficiency and agility in a company. How? By picking the right areas to apply agility.

If you try to be agile *everywhere* in your organization, you are likely to be agile *nowhere*. In addition, you don't want to disturb your efficient and consistent processes, which you've worked so hard to build, by introducing too much adaptability and variation. By choosing specific areas of focus, you can learn *what* you need to learn, and adapt *where* you need to adapt, while still retaining efficiency and consistency in areas where those are important.

So, how do you pick the right areas in which to focus your agility?

I developed the Setili Agility Framework, which you can access in Chapter 1 of my book *The Agility Advantage*, or at *www.setili .com/frameworks*, to answer this question. Using this framework, you can determine which areas of your business need the most agility, and which can be allowed to remain stable and consistent. The Framework, pictured in Figure 2.1, has two axes. The x-axis measures the speed and degree of change in the business environment, and the y-axis measures the impact of each part of your business on the customer's decision to buy.

The areas of your business that need the most agility reside in the top right quadrant, where both of these elements are high—that is, where the business environment is changing fast and there is a great impact on the customer's decision to buy. These are the areas that offer the greatest potential for growth, and that require the most-responsive, adaptable approach. Therefore, apply the new rules for fearless growth in these "top right quadrant" areas first to enhance your agility where it will be most valuable. Other parts of your business (the other three quadrants of the diagram) can remain focused on efficiency and consistency, and can take a slower approach to implementing the new rules.

Figure 2.1:

The Setili Agility Framework:

Which Elements of Your Business Require the Most Agility?

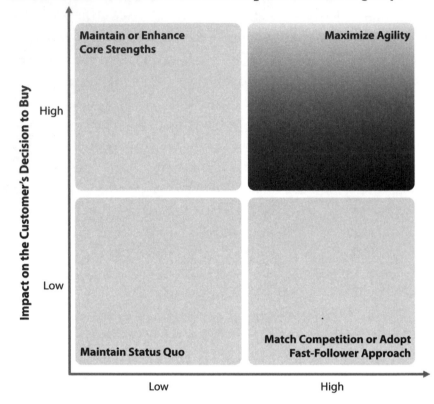

Speed and Degree of Change in the Business Environment

When You Need Agility, Deploy Focused Teams

When you are operating in the top right quadrant of Figure 2.1, consider assigning a dedicated cross-functional team to achieve your business objectives in a fast, adaptable way. Isio Nelson, senior vice president of emerging and differentiated services at Equifax, says:

> If you're operating in a fast-moving market, you need to act quickly when you spot a new opportunity. You want to get a minimum viable product into the hands of your target

customer, so that the customer can help you to innovate effectively. You need fast feedback from the customer, and you need to be able to promptly take action on that feedback. In a big company, however, it can be difficult to move as fast as you would like, because you have to coordinate across multiple organizational units. What we've found works well is to create a small, focused, cross-functional team to go after these opportunities. We try to protect the team from some of the big-company activities and policies that might slow them down. We don't want them to have to "ask permission" to do what they need to do to achieve our growth objectives.[14]

When you create a small, focused team, you want to provide access to all the great things the big company can provide—things such as customer relationships, company assets, funding, distribution channels, and the like—but you also want to protect them from having to ask permission too often.

Granting "special privileges" to these teams can accelerate their learning and progress, and enable fearless growth. Here are some approaches I have seen work well:

- Faster processes for approving expenditures, and lenience on investment approval hurdles.
- Freedom to focus on "learning objectives" and other non-financial metrics, as opposed to strict financial targets.
- Explicit "permission to fail" on experiments or initiatives.
- Flexibility on legal requirements. For example, instead of having an iron-clad contract with customers, a simple handshake agreement might suffice, so the two companies can quickly try new things, collaborating together to learn.

- Permission to not attend quarterly business reviews, weekly staff meetings, routine training classes, or other events that are not directly aligned with the team's mission.
- Permission to bypass internal processes that slow down action and learning.
- Access to outside experts.
- Lenient travel budgets.
- Greater latitude to hire (or terminate) team members.
- Different rules for how the team interacts with customers. For example, permission to call on existing accounts without having to ask the account manager's permission.
- Leeway to use marketing materials that are not fully buttoned up and formalized.
- Time to explore industries, companies, technologies, and ideas that are not directly related to your business (seeing how things are done in a completely different industry does wonders for creative thinking).

Create Systems to Enhance Flexibility

Most companies have design standards for their products and are very protective of their extremely valuable brands. For example, the Coca-Cola Zero Brand Identity and Design Standards document is 146 pages, and it spells out in great detail how the product is to be presented to the public. It is the brand bible for that product.

Regardless, Coca-Cola allows its customers to customize beverage marketing materials for their retail or foodservice outlet using an app that runs on most any platform—from desktop computer to smartphone to tablet—called Design Machine. According to the Coke website, Design Machine allows customers to create high-quality, customized beverage marketing materials in a matter of minutes. Any Coca-Cola customer, anywhere around the world, can design local marketing collateral that keeps the things that have to stay consistent, yet gives total flexibility to the local team to change the things that they are allowed to change. You can't, for example, change the specific color of red that is a part of the Coke brand, but you can change the price of the item you're promoting.

Coke created this system to enable local teams and customers to flexibly adapt to changing local conditions on the fly. As a result, the company is protected from some of the uncertainties of its far-flung global markets.

In Conclusion

Realize that there are elements in your business environment that are uncertain, but that sometimes this uncertainty, if you're good at managing it, can provide you with exciting new opportunities. Moreover, the ability to manage uncertainty well can be a tremendous competitive advantage. Pinpoint which parts of your business are most uncertain, and therefore require the greatest agility. In these areas, deploy focused teams, and give them the flexibility to adapt as they learn, and as the business environment evolves.

- **Don't fear uncertainty, embrace it.** People are hard-wired to fear uncertainty, but embracing uncertainty is key to growth and innovation. Be aware of common biases, discuss them as a team, and make them visible, so that you can deal with uncertainty in a more rational and fact-based way.
- **Make uncertainty work for you.** Uncertainty creates opportunities to pull ahead of the competition. Having the right risk mentality and moving quickly gives an advantage over competitors that are slower to respond.

- **Learn from the film industry.** Place multiple small bets. Repeat past successes. Keep budgets realistic and proportionate to projects. Target niche customer groups that you can uniquely please.
- **Manage risk in uncertain environments.** Communicate and rely on a buddy system. Talk about potential scenarios and how you will handle them before they occur. Anticipate and plan for what could go wrong.
- **Achieve efficiency *and* agility.** Agility is most needed in those parts of your business that have a large impact on the customers' decision to buy, and in which the business environment is changing fast. Apply the new rules for fearless growth to these parts of your business first, because these are the areas in which responding effectively to market change is most valuable.

3

Rule #2: Get in Sync
With Customers

Companies have long solicited and used feedback from their custom-ers to affect the decisions they make, from what new products to bring to market, when and for whom, what features to offer, and much more. However, although most businesses seek customer feed-back, it can often arrive late or not at all.

Nissan, the world's fourth-largest automaker, has made a com-mitment not just to seek customer feedback, but to accelerate the flow of information, opinions, ideas, and gripes directly from the customer to the people in the company who can improve the cus-tomer's experience.

Says Fred Diaz, Nissan division vice president and general man-ager, North America Trucks and Light Commercial Vehicles, "We're working to provide dealers immediate, actionable feedback from the customer on a real-time basis . . . while the customers are still in the store, or . . . within hours of them leaving the store. . . . The weeks or months that traditional customer satisfaction processes have typically taken—we all know it's far too late."[1]

Although automakers have long sought feedback from their customers, most often in the form of after-the-fact customer satisfaction surveys, they are commonly gathered by third parties, and it may take weeks, or even months, for the data to be compiled and shared. In addition, when the information finally does arrive, it may not make its way to the person, team, or department that can make the needed changes or spark new ideas for products, services, and other offerings.

Through its significant presence on Facebook, Twitter, and Instagram, Nissan receives a huge amount of feedback from its customers, fans, and detractors alike. The company currently has 702,000 followers on Twitter, more than 17 million followers on Facebook, and 1.2 million followers on Instagram. Nissan responds on a continuous basis to comments customers and others make on social media. The team that heads this effort happens to be in Nissan's marketing department, but it could be anywhere in the organization. It not only responds to individual customer comments, but it feeds that information *immediately* to the relevant dealer, engineering group, manufacturing plant, or customer service rep. These are the folks on the ground, the doers in the organization who can fix the customer's problem or spot opportunities to create new forms of value for the customer.

According to Scot Cottick, senior manager of digital and social media marketing at Nissan North America:

> Nissan's fans are very passionate and share amazing content with us. We've learned a lot from them and we're always encouraging them to share their stories, experiences, and photos with us. . . . Nissan consistently has the fastest response rate and responds to the highest proportion of fan comments compared to our competitors.[2]

By establishing this fast-feedback loop, Nissan has created a rich, two-way street with its customers. Nissan has become remarkably responsive to the market, and everyone in the company (not just marketing), is more aware of evolving customer needs.

A company's customers are a vast and underutilized resource. Too often, customer transactions are "one way"—the customers pay, and the companies provide a product or service in exchange. By fostering ongoing, two-way exchanges of information above and beyond the simple buying-and-selling transaction, companies can gain tremendous competitive advantage in a variety of aspects of their businesses.

Here are just a few ways that customer collaboration can enable your company's growth and agility:

- Customers often see trends and market changes on the horizon that companies cannot.
- Collaborating with customers enables you to discover synergies between your businesses that would otherwise be difficult to spot.
- Customers are your best marketers, referral sources, and advocates—speeding the process of acquiring new customers and closing sales with existing customers.
- You can often learn faster from customers than you can from your own internal teams.
- Learnings from collaborating closely with one customer can be applied to many other customers who have similar needs.

In this chapter, I'll explore how some of today's most successful businesses co-create with their customers by collaborating with the *right* customers, enabling customization, looking at outliers and edge cases, and more.

Customer Collaboration Enables Fearless Growth

A couple years ago, my husband, Rob, and I received an email message from outdoor gear retailer REI, the largest consumer co-op in the United States. The email started by thanking us for being among REI's best co-op members in Atlanta. That we were among REI's best members didn't surprise us; Rob and I are frequent shoppers at REI. What surprised us was what the email offered: the opportunity to meet with the company's CEO, Jerry Stritzke.

It is not every day that you get an invitation to meet with the CEO of one of the nation's most successful companies. But in keeping with REI's unique, outdoor-centric culture, the event wasn't going to be held in some sterile hotel conference room downtown. Instead, we would join the CEO for a 3- to 4-mile urban hike, a lesson in outdoor smartphone photography, introductory trail yoga, and refreshments. Midway through the hike, the group would stop for a one-hour round-table discussion with the CEO. The aim, the email said, was to re-create the energy that happens around a campfire. The event was designed to gain fresh ideas from customers in a relaxed setting specifically designed to heighten the flow of creativity. And not just from *any* customers, but from the company's *best* customers, the ones that REI considers to be most valuable to the brand, and to its future.

Co-creation and collaboration with customers enables fearless growth, as customers can help organizations innovate and transform their product offerings and their own internal processes and practices.

Figure 3.1 on page 69 shows how this customer collaboration can speed up the innovation cycle. By involving customers in ideation and strategy setting, conducting joint experiments and pilots with customers, soliciting and acting on customer feedback, and reaching out to "your customers' customers" for insights and guidance, you can gain the information you need to grow fearlessly.

Figure 3.1:

Impact of Customer Collaboration on Speed of the Innovation Cycle

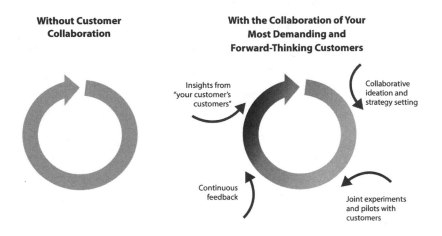

And what happens to businesses that fail to keep up with customer buying behavior and taste? They lose. Women's apparel chain The Limited failed to keep up with consumers' shift to buying online and preference for "fast fashion" retailers such as Zara, H&M, and Forever 21, which offer very low prices, and respond almost instantly to changes in customer buying preferences. In early 2017, The Limited announced that it would close all 250 of its U.S. stores and lay off 4,000 workers.

Choosing the Right Customers to Collaborate With

Of course, some customers are better to collaborate with than others, and when you're a large organization, the firehose of data that you receive from all your different stakeholders, potentially in the millions, can be difficult to manage. So, it's important to focus on the customers who have the greatest potential to give you the information you need to adapt to market change and prepare for the future. This means focusing on customers who are the most creative, demanding, forward-thinking, and interested in your business.

According to Eddie Yoon of The Cambridge Group, super-consumers—the people who are your company's greatest fans—average only 10 percent of the total customer base of most businesses, but they account for 30 to 70 percent of their sales, making them tremendously important. This makes it essential that you choose your customers wisely—attracting those who offer the greatest potential for increased earnings and knowledge.[3]

Safety is critically important for food companies, and they are always on the lookout for vendors who bring something new to the table. One of my clients is a specialty chemical company that wanted to become world class in food-safety-cleaning processes. To build this new line of business, they sought out customers who were similarly committed to continually upgrading this capability in their own businesses—collaborating with them to innovate new formulas, new equipment, and new operating procedures.

When you're a vendor, as this specialty chemical company is, your customers want you to be a fantastic supplier. They want you to bring the right chemicals, the right training, the right processes, and the right equipment so that their food will be wholesome and safe to consume. They want *you* to be the expert in food safety. Chipotle, perhaps, could have benefited from greater food safety expertise. When the company's food caused more than 500 customers to become ill in 2015, Chipotle experienced a 30-percent drop in quarterly sales and its first quarterly loss. And when new regulations or food safety practices come into being, it's in customers' interest to collaborate with you—the vendor—to quickly bring about the changes they need to comply. *The net result is that you both are fast together.*

The same thing happens in consumer markets in which customers volunteer to become early adopters of products and provide vital feedback to the manufacturer. Microsoft, for example, provides subscribers to its online version of Office 365 software suite the ability to opt-use the latest versions of Word, Excel, PowerPoint, and other popular programs before they are made available to the general public. The customers become, in essence, an army of beta testers who provide vital (and free) feedback to Microsoft to catch bugs and improve their products. Whether it's because they are frustrated with the product and want to make it better, or because they pride themselves in being "power users," these customers want to be among the first to try out the latest versions of the company's products and provide feedback to make them even better. Google and Facebook do the same thing by inviting their fans to try out new product offerings and provide feedback and suggestions for improvement. When Twitter CEO Jack Dorsey tweeted out the question "What's the most important thing you want to see Twitter improve or create in 2017?" he received thousands of replies within a day.

Your Most Dissatisfied and Demanding Customers Can Teach You the Most

As you select customers to collaborate with, it's important not to focus only on customers who love you, because those customers may keep you thinking everything is fine when it's really not. Although it may not be as pleasant as hearing the accolades from your happiest customers, you should pay a lot of attention to the complainers, the customers who leave you for a competitor, the customers who are very demanding, and the ones who don't like your product. The feedback you receive from them has the potential to be even more valuable than the feedback you receive from your fans.

Demanding and dissatisfied customers are often the people who understand your product the best. They may use your product in a more demanding application that really "puts it to the test." Who better to tell you what you can do to enhance your product beyond what you've previously envisioned? They could be your first harbingers of ill winds growing in your markets. If you can find out what they're unhappy about, why they're unhappy about it, and how it's removing value from their experience, then you've got feedback that's valuable. As someone once said, a complaint is a gift.

A good example of paying attention to your most demanding customers is when Uber picked Pittsburgh and San Francisco to test its self-driving car program. Pittsburgh offered several advantages: First, Pittsburgh is a typical American city, so the company was able to test the reactions of average Americans to driverless Ubers. Would the public embrace this new technology or reject it? Second, Pittsburgh is the home of Carnegie Mellon University, which is a key research center for driverless technology. Third, Pittsburgh is a city with a lot of curvy and steep roads—the ideal place to put the technology to the test.

When Uber chose San Francisco as the next city to begin testing its self-driving cars, the company was at least in part looking to acquire discerning technical people as customers. San Francisco's demanding physical environment with its steep hills, cable cars, and other potential obstacles was another plus.

Five Ways to Better Collaborate With Your Customers

Collaborating with your customers provides you with a valuable avenue to achieve fast, fearless growth. Not only do you provide your customers with real value, but they provide you with insights and opportunities far greater than the revenues and profits you derive from doing business with them. Here are five ways to better collaborate with your customers and to fine-tune your customer experience.

1. Make It Easy for Customers to Contribute

Recognize that customers are willing to contribute an immense amount. In a traditional relationship, companies provide products and services, and customers pay for those products and services. Now, however, customers are willing to contribute far more than just money. They are willing to collaborate on strategy and product innovation; they are willing to provide advice and technical support to other customers, and to contribute referrals, videos, and reviews. Why are customers so willing to contribute? Often, it is because *customers gain real value by contributing.* They get the opportunity to shape products and services to fit their own needs. They meet other like-minded customers, and may build a network of peers. They enhance their own status and professional reputation. They gain access to knowledge and expertise. Companies that make it easy for customers to contribute, by creating platforms and customer communities, hosting events, creating customer advisory boards, and otherwise encouraging customers to get involved, can reap immense benefits.

Chapter 2 of my book *The Agility Advantage* provides a wealth of examples of the roles customers can play in your business, and you may also access a framework for identifying these roles at *www.setili.com/frameworks.*

2. Deliver New Value Frequently

By updating and improving your products and services frequently, or even continually, you gain the fast customer feedback that enables fearless growth. Patricia Rosenfeld, senior vice president of USIS Operations at Equifax, tells a story of how delivering new value on a two-month cadence allowed her team to improve the customer experience from "less than optimal" to "differentiated" for its automotive dealership customers.

When we implement a major process or product change, we break the work into small chunks. Our objective is to work only on things that can deliver new value to the customer within two months. By delivering new value on a frequent basis, we speed up the customer feedback cycle. This is how we attacked the problem of speeding up onboarding of new customers in the automotive industry. We offer auto dealerships consumer credit, employment, and income data to help them to manage risk when making auto loans to consumers. Before this project, when an auto dealership wanted to implement our solutions, the process was cumbersome and time consuming. We strategically chose our most dissatisfied customer and redesigned the onboarding process, step by step, delivering meaningful new value to this customer every couple of months. This step-by-step process enabled us to get fast feedback from our customer as we made changes to our internal processes. The key to our success has been shifting our focus to the customer and delivering new value to them every two months.

By using this approach, we went from providing a less-than-optimal customer experience to providing a truly differentiated onboarding journey for auto dealers. Customers who were previously dissatisfied have now transformed into our ambassadors. As a result, we've won new business and grown revenues.[4]

3. Build Fast Feedback Loops

Fast feedback is the prime enabler of fearless growth, enabling you to move faster, try more things, and experiment confidently. Keep pushing the frontiers of how you get information from customers, and how you speed up customer feedback loops. Consider the example of Nissan earlier in this chapter, which takes customer feedback through social media and sends it immediately and directly to the person, team, dealer, or manufacturing plant that can impact it.

When I worked as an engineer for Kimberly-Clark, we had a facility in our headquarters building where parents and babies could come in to play. Kimberly-Clark product developers wanted to see how the diapers looked right after they came off the child. They wanted to know which parts of the diapers leaked, depending on the shapes and activities of the children wearing them. They wanted to know how easy or difficult it was to change the diapers, and how the parents decided when the diapers needed to be changed. Having this play space right in the building provided product developers with very fast feedback loops to identify ideas for product improvements, and to quickly assess whether the improvements would achieve the goals.

4. See for Yourself

Instead of chartering grand insight groups that take months and months of research and customer interactions before they deliver results, which may turn out to be too little too late, company leaders can create faster feedback loops by personally being out in the market with the customers. If you're running the company, make sure that you spend the time to be on the ground level with your front line and with your customers to see what's going on for yourself.

When my husband and I needed to, sadly, buy a vehicle to trailer our ski boat, I picked up an issue of *Trailer Boats* magazine (now out of business) to begin my research. The magazine recommended the Mazda MPV—a short-wheelbase minivan that offered an upgraded 200 horsepower V6 engine, a high towing capacity for its class, a lower gear for pulling your trailer in and out of a boat ramp, and special suspension.

So, how was it that a Japanese minivan was recommended as the first choice by a magazine that you'd think would be much more likely to recommend a big, burly American-made pickup truck or SUV?

According to the story I heard, Mazda, headquartered in Japan, was looking for a new niche market in the United States. Someone in the company subscribed to *Trailer Boats* magazine, and company reps drove all around the United States to see for themselves how people were using vehicles to tow their boats. They came and saw for themselves. Then they used the knowledge they gained to create features and improvements that were targeted specifically at people who towed boats behind their vehicles.

To establish fast feedback loops with your customers, get out there. See what's going on. Talk to people. Find ways to observe people. Find ways to mix it up and see what customers are really doing and thinking.

With today's technology, you can collaborate with your customers without them even knowing it. Companies are increasingly using the internet to gather information on how, when, and where customers use their products, and then use this information to fine-tune product offerings or add new features or improvements. Coca-Cola, for example, has begun implanting RFID microchips in Coke bottles that can track their movement, and John Deere's large farm tractors and other equipment are able to connect and share data with each other, as well as with owners, operators, dealers, and presumably John Deere itself. This system keeps tabs on the productivity of the machines, and actively tries to optimize their efficiency, while reducing downtime.

5. Act Quickly on the Feedback You Receive

When you receive feedback from your customers, move quickly to take any needed action before the information you have gained becomes stale, or even obsolete. I have observed that it often takes companies years to act on feedback they receive from customers. Sometimes this is unavoidable. For example, if new facilities need to be built, or complex technology infrastructure needs to be upgraded, the process can be lengthy. However, if it takes you years to act on the feedback you have received from customers, there is a good chance that the changes you have worked hard to implement will no longer be relevant to them. Therefore, try to respond in months, or even just weeks or days, to the feedback you receive, to get in sync with customer needs.

Tesla's Elon Musk recently modeled the power of acting quickly on customer feedback when a disgruntled customer sent him a tweet. The customer had stopped at a Tesla Supercharger recharging station on the way to a meeting in Palo Alto. When he arrived at the Supercharger, all the spaces were already in use and five other cars were in line. The customer noticed that the drivers had left their cars unattended in the spaces, and had apparently stepped away to run errands at a local coffee shop or grocery store, even though their cars had already finished charging. The customer tweeted his complaint directly to Elon Musk.

According to the customer, Musk personally responded to his tweet within minutes. Musk's tweet read, "You're right, this is becoming an issue. Supercharger spots are meant for charging, not parking. Will take action."[5]

In less than one week, Tesla *did* take action, introducing a fleet-wide idle fee for cars that remain parked at a Supercharger station after the car is fully charged. When a car's charge cycle is nearly complete, the Tesla driver is notified via the Tesla phone app. He or she then has five minutes to retrieve the car, or be subject to the idle fee of 40 cents per minute.

Create Customer Value and Insight by Enabling Customization

In-N-Out Burger is a throwback to a much earlier time in the fast-food industry. Founded in 1948, and one of the very first restaurants with drive-through service, In-N-Out has earned a level of customer loyalty that any business would envy. Although competitors such as McDonald's, Jack in the Box, and Wendy's rolled out menus loaded with items that were as far away from their central mission of serving burgers and fries as you could possibly imagine (including Caesar salads, chicken wraps, baked potatoes stuffed with broccoli and cheese, teriyaki bowls, and even yogurt with fruit and nuts), In-N-Out has stubbornly adhered to a simple menu with just three food items: hamburgers, cheeseburgers, and French fries.

However, hidden beneath this Spartan menu there lies a "secret" (actually, not so secret anymore) menu that allows customers to extensively customize their burgers and fries. Just a few of the items on the secret menu include animal-style fries (French fries smothered in melted cheese, grilled onions, and secret sauce), a 4×4 burger (four beef patties and four slices of cheese), and the Flying Dutchman (two slices of cheese melted between two hamburger patties—no bun or other additions).

Not only does the customization of In-N-Out's secret menu create an air of mystery while stoking the loyalty (and the Instagram accounts) of its customers, it provides vital insights to the company about its customers—what they like, and what they want to see more of.

Other, more-recent burger chains have played up the ability for customers to customize their burgers to their exact specifications—and have grown as a result. Five Guys Burgers and Fries, which has been touted by some as the East Coast equal to the West Coast's In-N-Out, proudly proclaims on its website that there are "over 250,000 ways to customize your burger"—primarily by selecting from their vast list of toppings, which include typical items such as lettuce, ketchup, and pickles, but also more esoteric add-ons such as grilled mushrooms, jalapeno peppers, and A.1. steak sauce.

Allowing customers to customize the products and services you sell to them enables you to learn what customers want. For example, Coca-Cola's computerized Freestyle soda fountain allows you to create hundreds of drink combinations by pushing different buttons for Coke products on a touchscreen—providing a dizzying array of possible options. Want an orange Coke? Simply press the Coca-Cola and Orange Fanta buttons. Or what about a Cherry Sprite Zero? No problem. A Minute Maid Raspberry Lemonade? Sure, why not?

Although the Freestyle is certainly a lot of fun to play with (and, according to Coca-Cola, it drives sales, with people 1.5 times more likely to recommend an outlet that has a Freestyle 7000 dispenser), all this customization also does something else: Coca-Cola is able to gather a tremendous amount of data on what customers like. All this data leads to insights that can be used by the company to develop new products and create brand extensions of existing products. If enough people, for example, consistently make orange Diet Cokes on Freestyle machines, then the company might try an official rollout of just such a product.

When you allow people to customize, you learn a lot about them, and you are able to innovate new products and new services and new ways of doing things that could potentially lead to future growth. Says Jennifer Mann, VP and general manager of Coca-Cola Freestyle, "Before Coca-Cola Freestyle, Caffeine-Free Diet Coke was available in less than 1 percent of our dispensers in the U.S. Now with Freestyle it's available in every dispenser, and it's become a top-five brand in the afternoon daypart. So, there was a huge unmet demand we were able to fill."[6]

When you enable your customers to customize your products and services, it's important to make the customization as inexpensive as possible for your business. You don't want to end up creating a new system that adds low-value complexity and excessive cost to your process. Your customization capability needs to be designed so that customers can customize on their own easily, in ways that are valuable to them, so that your systems and employees can efficiently deliver the customized products and services.

McDonald's provides a good example of customization gone wrong. In 2014, the company rolled out its "Create Your Taste" burger customization program, complete with touchscreen kiosks. The program was axed just two years later, however, due to higher costs for franchisees (the system cost about $125,000 per location), more complexity for workers, slower service, and higher burger prices for customers. Not only that, but the customized burgers (and, later, chicken sandwiches as well) required their own prep area and could not be ordered through the restaurant drive-thru—a huge disadvantage.

In contrast, airlines have found ways to allow customers to customize their flight experience in all sorts of ways, without adding significantly to company costs or service complexity. In fact, these customized options are becoming profit centers in and of themselves, adding dollars to the airlines' bottom lines. When you start the process by buying a basic seat in coach class, you can decide if you want to pay more for a ticket that allows you to make schedule changes or is refundable. You can also decide if you want to pay extra for a seat with more space, or one that is close to the front of the plane—allowing you to beat the rush to the door when disembarking. You can also choose to pay for access to onboard Wi-Fi and a meal of your choice. United, for example, currently offers a chicken sausage egg skillet for $9.99 and a cheeseburger with a side of fries for $11.99. And many airlines now offer in-seat entertainment—providing you with the option of watching the film of your choice or your favorite cable TV channels on DIRECTV for an extra fee.

The airlines have taken what is basically just a seat on the aircraft, and found ways to allow their customers to customize it. You may have an entirely different array of options assigned to your seat than the person sitting next to you, which provides a more satisfying experience for you and your seatmate, while the airline learns about your preferences, and earns more money doing it. If, for example, Delta Air Lines discovers that 20 percent of customers on certain routes pay the extra money to upgrade to a better Delta Comfort+ seat, then the next time they outfit a new plane they're going to be much smarter about the number and spacing of seats they install.

As computers and the software that drive them become increasingly powerful, the largest companies now have the ability to be fast and agile while customizing on a mass scale. Says John Donovan, chief strategy officer and group president at AT&T Technology and Operations, "What if we can now take massive scale and turn it into agility? [In the past] with large scale you miss out on agility, personalization, and customization, but big data now allows you all three."[7]

Using data that it collects from 130 million AT&T mobile phone subscribers, along with data collected from two other companies, Clear Channel Outdoor—the largest billboard company in the United States—has the ability to know who is driving past one of its billboards, and in a split second serve them an advertisement that is customized to their own personal product preferences. If, for example, the system (called Radar) knows that you recently visited the Tesla automobile website on your smartphone, it could serve you an ad for the latest Tesla Model S as you approach the billboard.

Figure 3.2 depicts a process for implementing customizability in your business.

Customization enables customers to make more choices, which makes them happier, while it enables you to gain valuable insights from the choices they make.

Customizing the experience for different types of customers makes you fast because it cuts to the chase, giving customers exactly

Figure 3.2:

Implementing Customizability in Your Business

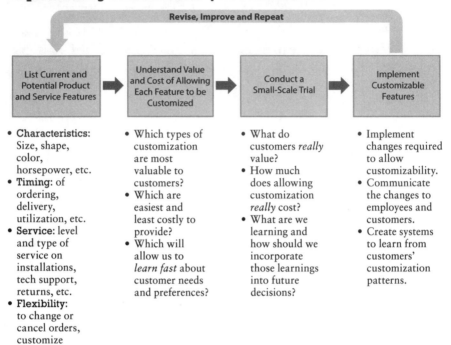

Revise, Improve and Repeat

List Current and Potential Product and Service Features	Understand Value and Cost of Allowing Each Feature to be Customized	Conduct a Small-Scale Trial	Implement Customizable Features
• **Characteristics:** Size, shape, color, horsepower, etc. • **Timing:** of ordering, delivery, utilization, etc. • **Service:** level and type of service on installations, tech support, returns, etc. • **Flexibility:** to change or cancel orders, customize during use, etc.	• Which types of customization are most valuable to customers? • Which are easiest and least costly to provide? • Which will allow us to *learn fast* about customer needs and preferences?	• What do customers *really* value? • How much does allowing customization *really* cost? • What are we learning and how should we incorporate those learnings into future decisions?	• Implement changes required to allow customizability. • Communicate the changes to employees and customers. • Create systems to learn from customers' customization patterns.

what they want earlier in the sales process so that they can say yes to the sale. Customizing also helps you grow, because a greater number of customers say yes sooner. Plus, when you give customers choices, you learn a lot from what they pick, and can continue to evolve your capabilities and offerings to match their needs.

No matter what business you are in, there are probably customizable products and services that you can offer your customers. It may be inefficient, however, to customize your offerings to every single customer you have. Not only will trying to accomplish this feat cost you more money, but it will slow down your organization. Marketers find that they can generally pare the number of buyer personas (representations of your ideal customers) to a handful, say three to five (depending on the nature of your business and your buyers, it could be more or fewer), that will capture about 80 percent of an organization's customers. The idea, then, is to create through research and data a set of personas that represent the majority of your customers, and then tailor your offerings to fit this set of personas, providing a manageable amount of customization while speeding your sales.

Observe and Cater to Outlier Customers to Gain Insights and Growth

In my book *The Agility Advantage,* I discuss the role of "outlier" customers—the customers who are using your products or services in unusual ways. Chances are the vast majority of your customers are using your products and services in the way that you originally intended, and in much the same way, day in and day out. There is a small minority of customers, however, that have found interesting new applications of your product or service that you hadn't thought of, or that you never intended.

Consider the example of the ubiquitous Kleenex tissue. Kleenex was introduced to the public by maker Kimberly-Clark in 1924 as the "Kleenex Sanitary Cold Cream Remover," marketed as a product for women to remove cold cream and makeup from their faces. And despite an advertising campaign that tried to link Kleenex with Hollywood stars, and as the "scientific way to remove cold cream," Kleenex was a dud in the marketplace.[8]

That is, until Kimberly-Clark's marketing team made the decision to talk with customers to find out if anyone had found other uses for the product. Traveling to Peoria, Illinois, the marketing people questioned customers, and they found out that almost two-thirds of them weren't using the product to remove their cold cream and makeup; they were using Kleenex tissues as disposable handkerchiefs. This discovery immediately led to a new marketing campaign for Kleenex, with ads that touted the product's health benefits. The new ads read,

"You use each tissue once—then destroy, germs and all." and suggested "Keep Kleenex Tissues in every room and in the car, too!"[9]

Think about some other ways that companies have built profitable new niches by looking at outliers and edge cases to spot harbingers of things to come.

- For years, Las Vegas casinos—with their "What happens in Vegas stays in Vegas" ethic of gambling, drinking, and entertainers such as Frank Sinatra, Liberace, and Dean Martin—catered almost exclusively to adults. This made sense because adults were the ones with the disposable income. However, at some point the casino industry realized that children (who were outliers to the core adult audience casinos were targeting) could also be a profitable market, bringing their gambling parents along with them. As a result, casinos increasingly catered to these outliers, building casino theme parks such as Circus Circus with its circus acts, Excalibur with its live jousting tournaments, Mandalay Bay with its huge wave pool and shark-filled aquarium, and New York New York—modeled after the skyline of New York City, complete with a facsimile of the Statue of Liberty and a roller coaster that runs in and out of the skyline at high speed.
- Eagle Creek started out making lightweight backpacks and travel gear for adventure travelers. The company saw that everyday people were using its light and durable equipment to satisfy their vacation, business, and other general travel needs, so they have since branched out to producing and selling lightweight and durable luggage, duffels, everyday bags, packing organizers, and more. I purchase Eagle Creek products frequently

because the company keeps coming up with better ways for me to stay organized as I travel. What was once a company devoted to a narrow niche of customers is now for everyone.

- L.L. Bean and Patagonia will take back products that fail to perform to the satisfaction of customers—even years after they were purchased. You may think this is a money-loser for the companies, but it enables them to learn a lot about their most loyal outliers: people (perhaps extreme users) who have enough brand loyalty to use their products for many years, and who know that the company will accept the product back. Plus, they get to see where the product is failing, and what they can do to make it better. For example, if a certain factory is causing failures of the product under real-life conditions, then the company knows to take a close look at the production process, or simply not to use that factory in the future.

- The Lotte New York Palace hotel in Manhattan understands that some of its customers love their dogs so much that they bring them along wherever they go. So, for these outlier customers, the Palace made an offer that catered just to them, providing up to two canine companions for each customer with their own leash and bed. In addition to the leash and doggie bed, the Lotte New York Palace included personalized food and water bowls for customer dogs, epicurean dog biscuits served each night at turndown, a custom canine room service menu, a complimentary 30-minute walk with a professional dog walker, and more. This kind of unique offering benefits the hotel in many ways. It makes for a more loyal (human) customer, while attracting an entirely new

set of dog-loving customers who are seeking a luxury
hotel experience they can share with their dogs.

When you deal with the same types of customers, buying the same products, and using them the same way, every day, it's easy to be lulled into a smug confidence that you know everything you need to know about how your customers' needs are evolving over time. In addition, market research and management reporting systems are notorious for "averaging" all customers together, blending specific needs into a bland summary of general information. As a result, critical information about outlier customers often gets lost in the mix and companies lose out on valuable insights about customer needs. Companies focus product and service enhancements on the "average" customer, and as long as she's pretty happy, they think they're doing well.

This is a risky assumption.

When we ignore the unusual customers, the ones at the edges of the bell curve, we miss important market signals. These "outlier" customers are those who do things a little differently. They may use our product or service in an unusual way, perhaps even in a way that's never occurred to us.

Why is this important?

Observing how outlier customers use our products gives us a window into emerging market trends and the future of things to come. A company I know noticed that a few of its customers frequently asked for rush shipments. The shipping department thought of these customers as a nuisance. One employee even admitted that she hesitated to pick up the phone when she saw their numbers on caller ID. But one day, a curious employee decided to look into this phenomenon.

She talked with these demanding customers, especially those who seemed willing to pay almost any price to get the product they wanted overnight. What she learned astonished her coworkers, and herself. These customers were modifying the products and then reselling them at a much higher price to overseas customers. This revelation sparked a flurry of creative thinking within the company.

The company set up a special process for no-hassle rush shipments. Soon, the company found other, similar customers, and these highly profitable sales took off, fueling growth for years to come.

To spot outlier customers, look for those who:

- Use your product in an unusual way, or under extreme conditions.
- Seem to get unusual value from your product or service (often, but not always, indicated by higher margins).
- Have gone to extra trouble to acquire your product, or have surmounted an obstacle to using it.
- Care a lot about a product characteristic that your company doesn't consider important.
- Need much less or much more service and attention than average.
- Are achieving fast growth.
- Are struggling or losing market share (especially if your product may be able to help).
- Operate in a particularly risky or fast-changing industry.
- Modify or combine your product with another, or use only a part of your product.
- Add value to your product and resell it.
- Are using your product in a geography or market that your sales channel does not serve.
- Are particularly innovative and forward-thinking, or are trendsetters.

Taking a closer look at your outlier customers and their behaviors can reveal how your product or service can solve customer problems in ways you may not be aware of. Sometimes this is the small nudge you need to spot a new market opportunity. Unusual customers are often your most profitable customers, so it's well worth your time to find them and leverage what you learn to grow your business.

In Conclusion

Most companies think of customers mainly in financial terms, particularly as sources of revenue, and ultimately, profit. However, customers provide much more value to your business than just the dollars and cents they inject into your organization. Collaborating and co-creating with your customers can enable your organization to grow fearlessly. As you work to build closer relationships with your customers, creating a rich, two-way street with them, be sure to keep the following points in mind:

- **Customer collaboration enables fearless growth.** When you collaborate with customers, you speed up the innovation cycle and gain insight into changing needs. Customers are willing to contribute an immense amount of material in the form of product improvement ideas, technical support for other customers, videos, reviews, and other content related to your products, referrals, and other marketing value. All of these contributions enable you to stay in sync with customers, which mitigates risk and leaves you better prepared for whatever the future may bring.

- **Choose the right customers to collaborate with.** Some customers are better to collaborate with than others. Focus your collaboration efforts on those customers who have the greatest potential to give you the information you need to adapt to market change and prepare for the future, including those who are the most creative, demanding, forward-thinking, and interested in your business.

- **Try these five ways to enhance collaboration.** You can collaborate better with your customers by recognizing how much they are willing to contribute, delivering new value often, building fast feedback loops, seeing for yourself, and acting quickly on the feedback you receive.

- **Create insight by enabling customization.** When you allow your customers to customize the products and services you sell, you are able to learn a lot about them, which can give you the information you need to innovate new products and services and ways of doing things, and stimulate growth. Design your customization capabilities to deliver the most value to customers, and the greatest insight for your company, at the lowest cost and least internal complexity. Identifying a limited number of buyer personas that capture the majority of your customers is one tool to do so.

- **Observe and cater to outlier customers to gain insights and growth.** Outliers—that is, customers who are unusual, or who use your products and services in unusual ways—can provide you with a window into emerging market trends and ideas for new products and services. What is only a niche customer group today may be a mass market in the future. Identify your outlier customers and recognize their value in generating ideas for future growth.

Rule #3: Partner, Borrow, and Share

Ideas are the lifeblood of most every business today, whether they originate from employees, vendors, customers, competitors, collaborators, or the public at large. Consider Amazon Prime. The idea for Amazon's "free" shipping program that provides two-day delivery on almost anything, for $99 per year, originally came from Amazon software engineer Charlie Ward, who suggested his idea through an electronic suggestion box within Amazon's internal website.

Building on Ward's idea, Amazon CEO Jeff Bezos held a brainstorming session in the boathouse behind his home in December 2004. The team came up with the name "Prime" and decided to price it, initially, at $79 per year, mostly because 79 is a prime number. "It was never about the $79 dollars. It was mainly about changing people's mentality so they wouldn't shop anywhere else," said Vijay Ravindran, who worked on the Prime team and is now the chief digital officer for the *Washington Post*.[1]

The Prime program has certainly changed *my* mentality. When I need something, I look at Amazon first. Amazon gives me all the information I need to make a good purchasing decision, and I value the extremely reliable two-day delivery that being a Prime member provides.

Surveys show that Prime members spend 2 to 4.6 times more than non-members.[2] Perhaps more important, Prime members spend more, and *become more satisfied*, with every year of membership. As a result, the Prime program has become one of the primary drivers of Amazon's success, with 46 million members globally, and 57 percent of Amazon's North American revenue coming from Prime members.

Of course, employees are not the only source of ideas. Starbucks gets a steady stream of ideas (47,737 at the time of this writing) from its customers via a website specifically designed for this purpose: MyStarbucksIdea.com. Many customer ideas have made it into practice, including cake pops, free Wi-Fi access, and those little green drink stoppers that keep the coffee in your cup when you're in motion.

These novel ideas—from an employee, in the instance of Prime's invention, and from customers, in the innovations at Starbucks—illustrate the weight of intellectual capital. Intellectual capital (a company's valuable knowledge, data, methods, processes, people, and relationships) has become far more important for business success than factories, buildings, or capital equipment. The generation and execution of new ideas form the basis for business innovation, more than a focus on the production of physical products or the expansion of offices in many locations.

The popular photo-sharing service Instagram was founded in October 2010 by two Stanford graduates, Kevin Systrom and Mike Krieger. Within just two months, the service had attracted 1 million users, and by September 2011, the number of users mushroomed to 10 million. In December 2011, Instagram was named the iPhone app of the year, and during the next three months, its user count reached 27 million. In April 2012, less than two years after the company was launched, Instagram was acquired by Facebook for $1 billion dollars.

But Instagram wasn't a huge company with offices and facilities scattered across the globe and millions of dollars of capital equipment squirreled away in plants and warehouses, churning out products at a dizzying clip. When Instagram was acquired by Facebook, the company had just 13 employees, each of whom became multimillionaires quite literally overnight. The company not only had very few employees, it had zero revenue. Today, there are more than 600 million active users on Instagram, and Credit Suisse analysts estimate that the company generated $3.2 billion in revenue to Facebook in 2016.[3]

Create Something From Nothing

The Instagram story illustrates how companies can create immense value, despite having few people and almost no physical assets. Advances in digitization, sensors, computing power, data storage, networking, and the interoperability of software systems now enable us to create "something from nothing." A small group of people can bring an idea to fruition and gain a massive user base with very little cost and at an astonishing speed. Andrew Hessel, distinguished research scientist at software company Autodesk, explains, "The gap between science fiction and science is getting really narrow now, because as soon as someone has that idea and articulates it, it can be manifested in a very short period of time."[4]

Companies that are successful in today's hyper-connected, hyperspeed world are those that travel light, relying on intellectual capital, such as talent, knowledge, data, and relationships, rather than hard assets, as a source of innovation and growth. By allying with partners, crowdsourcing, and collaborating with others outside your company, you can create new businesses and enter new markets, which would not be possible to access on your own. By developing more porous boundaries, you can share and grow your knowledge, talent, technology, and assets. You can become more agile and adaptable, thriving in times of great market change.

Partnering and collaborating with others allows both companies and individuals to accelerate their innovation and move rapidly from idea to execution.

Travel Light

For established companies, the speed with which ideas can be executed presents both a dangerous threat, and also an exciting opportunity.

In times past, a company's assets were a primary source of power and longevity. Now, however, many companies find that physical assets are burdensome, an impediment to agility and a drag on growth. Inventory can fast become obsolete, plants and real estate are difficult to sell when they are no longer needed, and information technology is easier to use and maintain in the Cloud than to own outright. Assets can weigh companies down when they want to move fast.

Similarly, having a large number of employees can slow companies down. To change direction, accelerate or decelerate requires tremendous effort and often money. There are organizational structures that have to be adjusted, processes that have to be reengineered, and people who have to be communicated to, trained, and redeployed. Being big tends to make it hard to change, whether it's to speed up, to slow down, or to change direction.

Just look at sharing economy companies: Most have no physical assets and few employees. DogVacay has no facilities, but arranges dog boarding by matching dog owners with people who would like to enjoy the company of a dog for a short while. Getaround owns no cars, but connects owners who can do without their car for a time with people who would like to use it. JustPark owns no driveways, but matches commuters looking for affordable parking options with homeowners who have extra driveway space they would like to rent out.

Create Flow in and out of Your Company's Borders

Big businesses *can* move quickly and with tremendous agility when they focus on developing their intellectual capital and on putting their best ideas into practice faster than the competition. China's Huawei Technologies, one of the world's largest telecom equipment makers, has enjoyed extremely fast revenue growth for years (more than 30 percent compound annual growth rate), in part because of its heavy investment in intellectual capital: Half of its 150,000 employees work in the research department.[5]

There's a rub, however. Intellectual capital is more valuable than ever, but it's also more perishable. Product life cycles are shortening, knowledge becomes outdated quickly, and patents provide little protection. Differentiation lasts only as long as we keep adapting and improving.

To stay fresh, and to keep building our intellectual capital, we need to increase the flow in and out of our corporate boundaries, to collaborate with others *outside* our company to build new ideas, new knowledge, and new capabilities.

Increasing the flow of talent, data, assets, technology, and knowledge into and out of our company can be risky. Company leaders worry that they may lose control of assets, that valuable intellectual property may be lost, and that it may be inefficient and cumbersome to collaborate with outsiders. All these fears are legitimate and rational, but the fact is: If managed well, this flow into and out of your company enables your growth and reduces your risk.

By working with partners, leveraging crowdsourcing, and using freelancers, companies can have a big footprint in the world today with fewer people, less assets, and less of everything. And companies that stay asset-light and employee-light are often better at moving fast and adapting quickly when the market changes. In a *Fortune* article, Geoff Colvin explained, "The 21st century corporation really is different. It operates in the friction-free economy, a world in which labor, information and money move around easily, cheaply and almost instantly. Companies are forming starkly new, more fluid relationships with customers, workers, and owners, and are rethinking the role of capital (as traditionally defined), finding they can thrive while owning less and less of it."[6]

In a fast-changing world, we can no longer rely only on the relationships, people, data, assets, technology, and knowledge that are inside our company. We must develop porous company boundaries and reach outside our company to share and collaborate with others. This strengthens the people, processes, and capabilities *inside* our company, and enables us to leverage the ideas and capabilities *outside* our company. Reaching outside enables us to commercialize our ideas faster, more easily, and with a lower cost.

Enabling these flows in and out of our company mitigates the complacency and inertia that can develop when we are constantly focused inside the four walls of our business. As Harvard Business School professor Michael Tushman explains it, when a management team is highly aligned, they become very inwardly focused. A priority is placed on operating within the existing policies; maintaining existing systems, procedures, and relationships; and preventing upsets. Inertia sets in. The team may fail to notice, or notice, but have trouble mobilizing quickly enough when changes in the external business environment occur.[7] Reaching outside the company for new ideas shakes up our thinking, and gets us out of mental ruts.

We need to allow information, ideas, and people to flow *both in and out of our borders*, but as John Hagel III, John Seely Brown, and Lang Davison explain in *Harvard Business Review*:

> We can't participate effectively in flows of knowledge—at least not for long—without contributing knowledge of our own . . . participants in these knowledge flows don't want free riding "takers"; they want to develop relationships with people and institutions that can contribute knowledge of their own. This is a huge hurdle for most executives who were trained to guard their knowledge carefully. Yet if they remain "takers" they will find themselves rapidly marginalized. Knowledge flows tend to concentrate among participants who are sharing with, and learning from, each other.[8]

Figure 4.1 on page 97 depicts the ways in which we can reach outside our corporate boundaries, to access—and share—talent, data, assets, technology, knowledge, and relationships across our company's borders.

Ideas Are Easy; It's the Execution That's Hard

The value of creative ideas, whether they are concepts for saving costs, increasing efficiency, or improving customer satisfaction, is undeniable. Still, even with a wide selection of innovation concepts, there exists a major problem in most organizations today: There are far *too many* ideas to act upon. In fact, there may be so many ideas coming into businesses from every possible stakeholder, via every sort of media, that they overwhelm the ability of executives and managers to assess and implement them, leaving many great ideas unexecuted. The result is billions of dollars worth of potential cost savings, new product ideas, process improvement ideas, and more passed over each year.

Figure 4.1:

Reach Outside Your Organization's Boundaries to Share and Collaborate With Others

This chapter is not about how to generate breakthrough ideas, a topic that I covered in some detail in my book *The Agility Advantage*. In this chapter, I consider how you can quickly take your idea from the drawing board to completed execution. I explore how companies have done this using internal resources, and how they have leveraged people and entities outside their walls through crowdsourcing, partnering, and more.

The Unbundled Company

As automation, artificial intelligence, and other technologies have shrunk the cost of operating a company, *Fortune*'s Geoff Colvin says, "Many companies are unbundling themselves, outsourcing functions to others, crowdsourcing R&D, and exchanging employees for contractors. A continual Hollywood model, in which people and resources come together to achieve a goal and then disperse to other projects, may become common across the economy. It's happening already."[9]

Companies can now grow large and have massive impact on the world with relatively few hard assets and few employees, provided they are open to relying on other businesses or individuals to help.

But when should we seek out partners? The easy decision is to outsource things that are not your distinctive competency—things that don't create a competitive advantage for you. Aspects of your business that are "commodities," the thinking goes, can be safely outsourced. For some, this means outsourcing manufacturing, call centers, or legal work to companies that are experts in doing these things reliably and efficiently. By outsourcing what is not our core source of differentiation, we free up time and management attention to focus on the things that really make the difference in our ability to attract and retain customers. We can also outsource things that are very central to our differentiation, provided we do it right.

Apple's business is designing, creating, and selling hardware—iPhones, iPads, iMacs, Apple Watches, Apple TVs, and more—but it outsources the vast majority of manufacturing of its hardware. Aside from a company-owned-and-managed factory in Cork, Ireland, all the company's manufacturing (representing hundreds of thousands of jobs) is offshored and outsourced to businesses (such as Foxconn and Pegatron) in China, Korea, Taiwan, Mongolia, and elsewhere.

By doing this, Apple surely saves only a few dollars per iPhone or tablet, but it gains something even more valuable: the ability to move much more quickly than if it manufactured its products in the United States.

According to one story, a little more than a month before the iPhone was scheduled to be launched in 2007, Steve Jobs suddenly made the decision to include a glass screen on the device instead of plastic, a prototype of which was easily scratched in his pocket. "I want a glass screen," a frustrated Jobs demanded, "and I want it perfect in six weeks."[10] Although the special, hardened glass was going to be manufactured by a U.S. company, Corning, large sheets of glass would have to be cut to size and then installed onto millions of iPhones. Unfortunately, there was no U.S. company that could meet the challenge of Jobs's ridiculously fast schedule.

When Apple approached U.S.-based companies, they were told that there was no possible way to achieve this requirement in just a few short weeks. So, Apple reached out to suppliers outside the United States and a Chinese firm rose to the challenge, building a dormitory to house 8,000 workers *before* even signing an agreement with Apple. As soon as the contract was signed, the Chinese factory began pumping out 10,000 glass-faced iPhones a day to meet Apple's requirement, and to allow Jobs to have the product he wanted, on the schedule he demanded.

If Apple had owned its own manufacturing facilities, it very likely would not have been able to make the abrupt change from plastic to glass screens in only six weeks. Outsourcing enabled the company to do what would have otherwise been impossible.

Engage Partners

You can create something entirely new by partnering with another organization that can bring something to the table that you don't have. You may have manufacturing and R&D, and they may have a distribution channel—or vice versa. They may have a distribution channel in Europe and you don't. Partnerships enable you to move with greater speed and agility to act on growth opportunities. In fact, it is often easier to start something new outside of your current organizational structure than to start it inside your current organizational structure.

Large businesses have become more efficient and agile by creating extensive global alliances and supply chains that allow them to focus on and optimize each piece of their business. In just one example, General Electric has turned to India to develop new healthcare products, and more than 25 percent of such products are now developed there. Why? Because development costs are significantly lower in India than in the United States. According to economist Pankaj Ghemawat, in 1980, the top 1,000 U.S. public companies derived only 1 percent of their revenues from alliances. In 2017, the top 1,000 U.S. public companies derive 40 percent of their revenues from alliances.

Multiply Your Impact by Setting a Clear Intent

In 2013, Elon Musk, CEO of Tesla and SpaceX, came up with a concept: a futuristic train that could transport riders from San Francisco to Los Angeles in just 35 minutes—at an average speed of around 600 miles per hour. He developed a rough plan for the idea, which he described as a "cross between a Concorde and a railgun and an air hockey table,"[11] and gave it a name: Hyperloop. Musk posted the idea on the web, and then invited anyone who wanted to contribute to the design and further develop it.

Before long, companies sprung up to take on the challenge, including Hyperloop One, TransPod, and Hyperloop Transportation Technologies. Each of these companies has put together a team of people to design and develop working Hyperloop prototypes. Hyperloop Transportation Technologies, for example, has enlisted a group of 500 geographically dispersed freelance engineers who are willing to work—not for a regular salary, but for stock options in the company. By setting the intent and putting his idea online for all to see, Musk set all these activities in motion.

As Musk famously said, "One great engineer will replace three medium ones." The ratio may be even greater when you consider one great engineer can move with lightning speed by leveraging the resources outside the company, and can give inspiration and ideas to many others in the company. The same holds true for *any* employee. One great production worker, product developer, human resources director, or marketing professional is similarly worth three—or more—medium ones in their ability to positively affect the organization and its results.

Use Collaboration Platforms

GitHub is a cloud service that programmers use to store and share their software projects, and work on them collaboratively, in teams. The site has more than 14 million users—none of whom are paid for the work they voluntarily do there. It's used by individual developers, small startups, and large companies such as Apple, Google, and Walmart. A company needing development resources can post a requirement on GitHub, and people who are qualified can come in and work on it when and where they like. In his book, *Thank You for Being Late,* Thomas Friedman describes that a developer takes out a piece of code, works on it, puts it back in, and then the next person can take that piece out, work on it, and put it back in. According to Friedman:

> A decade and a half ago Microsoft created a technology called .NET—a proprietary closed-source platform for developing serious enterprise software for banks and insurance companies. In September 2014, Microsoft decided to

open-source it on GitHub to see what the community could add. Within six months Microsoft had more people working on .NET for free than they had working on it inside the company since its inception.[12]

Hewlett Packard Enterprise uses the OpenStack software platform to, in the words of president and CEO Meg Whitman, "Leverage the community, and we have a hundred thousand developers who don't work for us—but what they can do in a week, we couldn't do in a year." Whitman continues, "I am convinced that the world is driven by validation and that's what makes these communities powerful. People are driven by their desire for others in the community to validate their work."[13]

Open-source platforms such as GitHub and OpenStack are a great way for people to collaborate with businesses. After all, what's better than that to have an employee who is volunteering to do something for you they actually like to do, and are good at?

Wikipedia works in much the same way. This online encyclopedia of information, which has made old-fashioned published encyclopedias obsolete, is mostly created and maintained by a vast, international army of volunteers. As of 2017, there are currently more than 5 million individual articles on Wikipedia, 70,000 editors, and 1,280 administrators. All volunteers.

In 2004, the Defense Advanced Research Projects Agency (DARPA) sponsored the Grand Challenge. The competition offered cash prizes to teams that could create a completely autonomous vehicle that could navigate a 150-mile off-road course in the Mojave Desert, from California to Nevada. No team successfully completed the challenge, with the Carnegie Mellon University team making it the farthest distance—7.3 miles.

The outcome of the 2005 Grand Challenge was much different. Held a year and a half after the 2004 Grand Challenge, the competition attracted 23 teams, all vying for the $2 million first prize.

Five teams successfully completed the course, with the Stanford University team capturing first-place honors with a time of six hours, 54 minutes.

The car companies couldn't build their own autonomous vehicles, but when the government put out the idea and offered a prize to the winner, this gave the process a tremendous jump-start. If you're trying to do something really new, you often need outside people or you can't do it.

Try Multiparty Innovation

Some large businesses today are creating partnerships through multiparty innovation. Cisco has developed something it calls CHILL, for Cisco Hyperinnovation Living Labs. These labs provide a forum for leaders of large, well-established companies to come together to seize opportunities that they are not able to on their own. This was the case when senior executives and innovation leaders from Airbus, DHL, Caterpillar, and Cisco met in Berlin to create partnerships that would lead to solutions to shared problems within six months.

In a recent *Harvard Business Review* article, authors Nathan Furr, Kate O'Keeffe, and Jeffrey Dyer explain, "Instead of relying on start-ups to create innovations and then buying into them, organizations taking part in this new process, which we call *ecosystem innovation*, collaborate to develop and then commercialize new concepts."[14]

Set Out to Create Tangible Value Within a Set Time Frame

David Lee, former director of innovation programs at SunTrust Bank, a bank with $8.7 billion in annual revenues, has long been concerned with the inability of some organizations to take the ideas they generate and sift out the good ones, and then implement them.

With this concern in mind, Lee created and implemented something at SunTrust he called Innovation Friday.

Innovation Friday is a one-day collaborative design session that invites employees from different backgrounds to explore a difficult problem, creating not just ideas but meaningful change in a 10-week period of time. According to Lee, the program was able to consistently produce real and tangible improvements to some of SunTrust's most vexing problems at little or no cost.

Says Lee, "We structured Innovation Friday to apply the thinking and talent that is already in the company," and to "give people a structure to solve problems quickly and collaboratively."[15] It is Lee's belief that innovation wants to happen everywhere, and knowing who can help you is 50 percent of any challenge.

Innovation Friday was centered around a three-step process specifically designed to move good ideas into practice:

Step 1: Choose a problem. Not an easy one, but not an unrealistic one. Says Lee, "We have tried to solve things like, 'We spend millions of dollars on technology, but it doesn't feel like we get our money's worth . . .' or 'How can we make this place more appealing to younger workers?' or 'Why don't people collaborate across geographic locations very well?' "[16]

Step 2: Find a sponsor, then find 30 people who will be willing to have an honest conversation. Explains Lee, "An executive sponsor's role is important. We need a champion to support the ideas that come out of the design session." The sponsor, Lee says, makes it very clear that the group has "permission" to think about *big* changes. That way, instead of being hemmed in by limitations ("Will they let us?") participants think expansively about the possibilities ("What if we . . .?" and "How might we . . .?"). Lee added, "Finding the right participants is

105

also critical. We need people who can see past the barriers that stand in the way of innovation. It's also important to bring in different perspectives on the problem. Be sure to bring in people from every side of the issue."[17]

Step 3: Set a date! Says Lee, "We like Fridays because it's easier for people to dress down and loosen up. Because we are asking for a full day (9 a.m. to 4 p.m.) you may need to schedule this six to nine weeks out. We also like to choose a musical playlist. Innovation should be something you can dance to!"[18]

Innovation Friday was divided by Lee into three separate acts:

Act 1: Explore (Friday morning). This act focused on learning about the problem (by way of a panel or "TED-like" speakers); getting tough truths out into the room (what is said in Innovation Friday stays in Innovation Friday); giving participants permission to think differently (bring in wild ideas from other places); and find the important themes (what keeps coming up over and over?). The problems developed by the group to tackle are posted around the room on big sheets of paper, and participants are invited to break into teams, standing under the problem they are most interested in solving.

Act 2: Imagine (Friday afternoon). This act focused on designing solutions (solutions should be doable in 10 weeks and for little or no cost); making pitches to the group (each team is given six minutes to present their solution to the group, and three or four are voted on to move to the next Act); and employees signing up on a team to put the solution into practice within 10 weeks.

Act 3: Attempt (10 weeks following Innovation Friday). Teams meet for an hour or two each week to explore ways the solution can be implemented. SunTrust assigned a program manager to each team to keep the team focused on what is feasible within a short period of time (which was often a lot).[19]

In addition to Innovation Friday, SunTrust implemented several other programs specifically designed to encourage employees to identify problems and take action as well as address problems and opportunities important to the bank. These programs include RISE (Rapid Innovation Special Event), a hackathon during which teams go from idea to working prototype in three weeks with no investment; Daylight, which takes the best RISE ideas and tries to implement them in 100 days; and Gauntlet, a business-plan competition in which teammates vie for the chance to get funding and implement their ideas by way of a *Shark Tank*–like event.

In one of the Gauntlet competitions, SunTrust offered four challenges that teams could choose from:

1. Use digital or mobile technology to make our people twice as effective.
2. Improve the onboarding experience for new clients.
3. Create a true 21st-century product—something that could not have existed 15 years ago, which is now possible.
4. If we give you $1 million dollars, can you turn it into $10 million in two years?[20]

According to Mark Pearson, SunTrust's senior vice president of strategy and innovation, results of these and other innovation programs at the bank included outreach to more than 10 percent of all teammates (2,500-plus), creation of a 100-plus person cross-enterprise team of innovation entrepreneurs, forward cost savings of $6 million a year, and projected net new revenue of $60 million over five years.[21]

Hold Pitch Contests and Hackathons

Michael Corbat, CEO of Citigroup, explains that his company is looking outside the walls of the financial institution—and across borders—to innovate and implement solutions that can advance the organization's goals. Says Corbat:

> While everybody has the ability to be a fast follower, we wanted to lead from the front whenever possible. We thought the right way to do that was not just in the U.S.—and in particular in Silicon Valley—but to make investments on the ground in places like Dublin, Tel Aviv, and Singapore in innovation that can benefit Citi across our businesses. That's why we established innovation laboratories in each of those cities, each with a particular focus.[22]

In one example of what Citigroup is doing to innovate and implement solutions to difficult problems, in Tel Aviv the company sponsored a pitch contest in partnership with the Israeli government. Current and prospective startups were invited to pitch their ideas to Citigroup. The company then provided several selected startups with a space in which to work, seed capital, and access to the bank's technology—everything they would need in order to implement their ideas. After six months, a new group of startups was invited to pitch their ideas, and the cycle started all over again.

According to Corbat, the contest was well worth the bank's investment of time and money. "Out of that effort, we helped advance a culture of innovation within our own firm. We get a lot of smart people coming through, some of whom we may even partner with on future projects."[23]

Consider how you can use contests, hackathons, and innovation laboratories to create new sources of innovation and execution.

Bridge the Old Economy and the New Economy

Southern breakfast staple Waffle House was recently looking for a way to get its foot in the sharing economy door. This was admittedly a tall order for a company known for its brightly lit restaurants, 24-hour service, and hash browns served eight different ways. Says Waffle House CEO Walt Ehmer, "We're just bacon and eggs over here. I've been amazed with the explosion of Uber and Airbnb and other technology that kind of enables people to get together and conduct business together."[24]

To make its entry into the sharing economy, Waffle House partnered with Roadie, a startup that matches people who have packages that need to be delivered with people who are driving that direction. According to Roadie, which aspires to become the Uber of package delivery, "By tapping into extra space in passenger vehicles already on the road, Roadie gives consumers and businesses a more flexible, cost-effective, and greener delivery service."[25]

And that's where Waffle House comes in. Instead of having Roadie drivers deliver packages door to door, the idea is for Roadie drivers and package recipients to meet at one of the 1,750 Waffle House restaurants across the country to hand off their packages. To sweeten the deal, Waffle House is offering a free drink and waffle to Roadie drivers who agree to complete their delivery at a Waffle House.

Although it may be some time before this new partnership between old- and new-economy businesses becomes a threat to the likes of UPS, FedEx, and the U.S. Postal Service, it's definitely a step in that direction.

Many Great Ideas Start Out as Mediocre, Problematic, or Crazy

In an interview, Peter Diamandis, entrepreneur and founder of the X Prize Foundation, explains that there are huge obstacles in taking new ideas in businesses and putting them into practice. "Most innovation dies inside companies if it's anything other than incremental, because it threatens the beast. The day before something is truly a breakthrough, it's a crazy idea. And crazy ideas do not survive well inside well-established companies."[26]

Although it's great to have a good idea, it's important to keep in mind that many ideas are ugly ducklings, starting out rather mediocre or problematic, and eventually becoming strong growth drivers.

Twitter was a network (originally called Odeo) for people to find and subscribe to podcasts. Starbucks got its start selling espresso makers and coffee beans, not coffee drinks. Pinterest was originally a site called Tote, on which people could shop their favorite online stores and create collections of their favorite products. And Instagram was at first an app called Burbn that was built around the multiplayer social network game Mafia Wars. Beauty products giant Avon originally started out selling books door to door.

The first idea that an employee, or anyone else, comes up with is likely not a fully formed, "ready for prime time" winner. But if you can create an environment that encourages people to collaborate, develop, hone, and improve each other's ideas, your ideas will take shape, and many will end up being very successful, once fully developed. And sometimes, the "idea" is merely the thought that "let's go out and find out what customers really want."

When you don't have a clear intent for your idea or a specific reason for it to be put into practice, then it's really hard to get people excited about it. When the intent is clear, on the other hand, it is easy to get other people to collaborate with you, which will increase the chance that your nascent concept will be improved upon and implemented.

Many companies that have grown very big, very fast have a strong idea that drives everything they do. Google's idea is to organize the world's information and make it universally accessible and useful. Facebook wants to give people the power to share and make the world more open and connected. And Amazon's idea is to be the Earth's most customer-centric company—to build a place where people can come to find and discover anything they might want to buy online. These ideas are elegant and compelling.

You may not have all the components of your idea to begin with (what you are going to offer, how, to whom, and at what price), but this should not stop you from pursuing the idea and filling out and fine tuning these components over time.

In his leadership book, *The Virgin Way*, Sir Richard Branson tells the story of two entrepreneurs, Matthew Bucknall and Frank Reed, who visited his office in 1997. The two presented a business plan that was about the most concise he had ever seen. It read, "We want to create the first global comprehensive consumer-led branded health and fitness facility—readily accessible to a wide socio-demographic group at a price consumers are willing and able to pay." There were a lot of unknowns. How would they be able to create a "comprehensive" club that would span the globe, yet could still be offered at a price that consumers are willing to pay? How could they create a club that would appeal to, and be accessible to, a wide socio-demographic group? How would they make the club truly "consumer-led"? All these unknowns didn't deter Branson. He liked the idea, and asked Bucknall and Reed to spend a year looking at what was happening in the health and fitness sector all around the world.

The two spent that year researching and planning, and in 1998 launched the first Virgin Active club in Preston, England. By 2012, the business had 300 clubs across the globe, 1.25 million members, and $1 billion dollars in revenue. It took time for the idea to take shape, but once it did, it took off.

There will always be naysayers, there will always be a million reasons to kill any good idea, but if you paint a picture of your intent, enlist others to contribute, and work around the problems, you will be able to shape your ideas to become valuable growth drivers.

In Conclusion

In the past, a company's hard assets such as manufacturing plants, warehouses, and industrial equipment were its primary source of power and longevity, but this is no longer the case. Assets such as these weigh down companies when they want to move fast. To move quickly and grow fearlessly, it's far better to travel light—developing partnerships and collaborations with others outside the organization. As you work to build partnerships and collaborations, be sure to keep the following points in mind:

- **Create something from nothing.** Focus on creating value from intellectual capital and ideas, rather than physical assets. Traveling light, with porous boundaries, helps companies be more agile and adaptable.
- **Create flow in and out of your company's borders.** Collaborate with others outside your company, leveraging partners and taking advantage of freelancers and contract workers. These fluid relationships allow for rapid adaptation when the market changes.
- **Unbundle your company.** Engage partners and outsource functions to others when possible. Work on a project-based format, with flexibility. Outsource things that are not your distinctive competency.
- **Engage the world through crowdsourcing and collaboration.** Using open-source platforms in which anyone can contribute is a great way to get new input. Multiparty innovation, with multiple companies coming together, increases the ability to create solutions.

- **Reach out both inside and outside your company.** Hold collaborative design sessions, pitch contests, and hackathons to generate new ideas, both from your employees and others outside the company.
- **Many great ideas seem mediocre, problematic, or crazy at the beginning.** When you sense that an idea has potential, identify the specific problems that need to be solved, and address them. With fine-tuning, even the craziest ideas can become strategic breakthroughs.

5

Rule #4: Connect and Strengthen Your Ecosystem

Salesforce was started by Oracle veteran Marc Benioff in 1999 in a one-bedroom apartment on Telegraph Hill in San Francisco, along with three programmers. Benioff's idea, which was revolutionary at the time, was to create and sell customer relationship management (CRM) software as a service (SaaS) over the internet using centralized servers to store client data instead of selling physical software to its customers. Benioff's company, Salesforce.com, would enable salespeople and organizations to connect with one another, track their contacts and conversations with customers, and perform a variety of other sales-related tasks. In 2000, about a year after it started up, Salesforce.com began selling its hosted CRM system to small business customers.

From its earliest years, Benioff saw the value in creating and fostering the growth of an ecosystem around the company—a universe of companies, products, and partners that exist because of Salesforce. As the company grew, Salesforce started something called a City Tour, which began as a six-stop event designed to create word-of-mouth marketing by having customers share their success stories with their peers. Each session lasted a few hours and highlighted the latest Salesforce products while providing opportunities for customers to network. Says Benioff about City Tour:

> The intent was to invite disparate groups—customers, potential users, analysts, press, partners, philanthropists, and nonprofit leaders—and allow them to interact and feed off of one another's energy and insights. Truthfully, we weren't sure whether or not all of these constituents would attend, but we decided it was worth a try.[1]

Much to the surprise of Benioff and his team, attendees weren't as interested in hearing from the Salesforce representatives at these City Tour events as they were from one another. Continues Benioff:

> We had assumed that we would field the questions, but instead our customers chimed in with the answers. Initially, we were surprised to find ourselves watching from the sidelines, as a group of 60 people suddenly broke off into a conversation about how to use our service. However, after seeing this unfold at event after event, we began to recognize what was happening: People weren't attending these events to meet us. They were coming to meet other people using the product.[2]

City Tour marked the birth of the Salesforce ecosystem. With the success of City Tour, and eventually World Tour (the international version of City Tour) in 2003 Salesforce started a much larger, multi-day event called Dreamforce. According to the company,

"Dreamforce brings together thought leaders, industry pioneers, and thousands of your peers for four high-energy days of fun, inspiration, networking, and giving back."[3] Dreamforce led to a massive expansion of the Salesforce ecosystem.

The first Dreamforce event had 1,000 registered attendees and took place at the St. Francis Hotel in San Francisco. By 2016, Dreamforce had grown to more than 171,000 registered attendees from 83 different countries, along with an additional 15 million live online viewers. Attendees were treated to 3,300 breakout and theater sessions, presentations by Mark Cuban, Melinda Gates, Tony Robbins, Billie Jean King, Representative John Lewis, Mary Barra, Sir Richard Branson, and others, and an exclusive concert by U2. Depending on who you believe, Dreamforce is either the first or second largest technology conference in the world.

According to Laura Fagan, "Salesforce was the first in the Cloud computing space to dream up a business model built on partnership. We recognized that our success hinged on building a vibrant ecosystem."[4] This ecosystem is divided by the company into four key segments:

1. **Customers.** About 1.8 million Salesforce customers actively participate in the company's Success Community, an online forum for customers to connect, ask questions, give advice to other customers, and provide feedback to Salesforce. The Salesforce IdeaExchange invites customers to suggest new features for products, and the company often responds by implementing the features in its three yearly product releases. The Salesforce MVP Program recognizes Success Community members who have gone above and beyond in their contributions.

2. **App store.** According to the company, the Salesforce AppExchange (launched in 2005, well before the Apple and Google app stores) is the number-one enterprise app

marketplace, with more than 3,000 different apps available for customers to install and more than 4.3 million downloads to date. More than 70 percent of Salesforce customers have downloaded and installed at least one app from AppExchange.[5]

3. **Partners.** Salesforce works with thousands of independent software vendors and developers, giving it the largest partner ecosystem of any technology company in the world. In addition, the company partners with consultants and systems integrators, and offers training, certifications, and other resources to its partners.

4. **Developers.** There are more than 2 million Salesforce developers, and the company provides them with a variety of development tools and services to make their jobs faster and easier. These include App Cloud services, drag-and-drop Salesforce Lightning Components, the Lightning App Builder platform, and the Trailhead learning platform.

In an article in *Forbes,* Jason Bloomberg writes, "And while other vendors have built flourishing ecosystems, to be sure . . . nobody has ever built an ecosystem bigger or better than Salesforce has."[6] The global economic power of the Salesforce network today is truly remarkable. According to an IDC white paper:

- Between the end of 2015 and the end of 2020, Salesforce and its ecosystem will enable the creation of more than 1.9 million direct jobs within the Salesforce customer base, along with an additional 2.8 million indirect or induced jobs.
- During this same period, the benefits of Cloud computing will add $389 billion in new business revenue, or GDP impact, to the local economies of Salesforce customers.

- The Salesforce partner ecosystem generates three to four times more revenue than Salesforce. By 2020, the Salesforce ecosystem will earn $4.14 for every $1 that Salesforce makes.
- Annual revenue for the Salesforce ecosystem will grow to more than $70 billion (in 2015, this figure was less than $20 billion).[7]

By building a very large, powerful, and valuable ecosystem, Salesforce broke the code on how to get salespeople to input data and then use the information gained to improve their sales efforts. Salesforce enabled this very collaborative group of people with common interests to share ideas and ways of managing the sales process. Salesforce made using the system fun, engaging, and rewarding for salespeople.

There are numerous examples of companies that have built powerful ecosystems that draw in customers, suppliers, vendors, communities, and the world. Amazon, Airbnb, and Uber are just a few examples. In this chapter, I explore ecosystems in more detail.

Building an Ecosystem Can Be a Leap of Faith

Fearless growth inevitably involves risk and exploring unfamiliar territory. Although you can work to control as many factors as possible, you certainly can't control everything.

NCR Corporation builds software platforms to connect its ecosystems of customers and partners in the financial services, hospitality, and retail industries. NCR's customers, which include banks, restaurant chains, and retailers, value the ability to easily connect to third-party mobile apps for ordering food, participating in loyalty programs, paying for products, and making restaurant reservations. These partners, in turn, value the ability to connect directly to NCR customers' systems for managing transactions, reservations, and other business processes. NCR seeks to attract the best partners to provide tremendous value to its customers. Nonetheless, NCR's software solutions chief of staff John Morrow says:

> Building an ecosystem is an act of dynamic co-creation. It can't be fully engineered; it must grow organically as well. You do whatever you can to enhance the value of your platform, and you work to attract the right customers, partners, and developers. No matter how well you develop plans, however, and no matter how well you execute on those plans, it remains in large part a leap of faith. You can't predict exactly how the ecosystem will take shape, who will join, and how they will interact with and do business with the other participants in your platform ecosystem. You have to be comfortable with ambiguity, because you enter uncharted waters daily.[8]

The Rise of the Ecosystem

According to the *Oxford English Dictionary*, an *ecosystem* is "a biological community of interacting organizations and their physical environment." James Moore coined the term *business ecosystem*. In his book, *The Death of Competition*, Moore defined a business ecosystem as:

> An economic community supported by a foundation of interacting organizations and individuals—the organisms of the business world. The economic community produces goods and services of value to customers, who are themselves members of the ecosystem. The member organisms also include suppliers, lead producers, competitors, and other stakeholders. Over time, they coevolve their capabilities and roles, and tend to align themselves with the directions set by one or

more central companies. Those companies holding leadership roles may change over time, but the function of ecosystem leader is valued by the community because it enables members to move toward shared visions to align their investments, and to find mutually supportive roles.[9]

It is no coincidence that many of the most successful companies being created today are companies with powerful ecosystems. This is a demonstration of what is known as the *network effect*, a situation in which a product or service grows in value as more people use it, and use it more often. Consider the example of Amazon.com, and its system of customer product reviews. In 1995 the company created a mechanism for customers to post reviews of the products they purchased on the site. According to one writer, as a result of Amazon's action, "Many people thought the Internet retailer had lost its marbles. Letting consumers rant about products in public was a recipe for retail suicide, critics thought."[10]

As it turned out, Amazon's idea was retail *gold*, and it led to a new way for people to shop for the products they wanted: by first reading reviews written by other customers. According to a recent Deloitte survey, 66 percent of shoppers who research products online say they read customer reviews on websites, and a survey by BrightLocal found that 88 percent of consumers trust online customer reviews as much as they trust personal recommendations.[11]

So, where do people go when they want to read a review of something they're about to buy? In many cases, to Amazon.com. And once they land there, there's a very good chance that they will buy the item from Amazon. A Stanford researcher created a dataset of all Amazon reviews for an 18-year period, from June 1995 through March 2013, and found that approximately 6.6 million users had written more than 34 million reviews for 2.4 million different products.[12] Millions of customer reviews have been added to the site since then.

In addition to customer reviews (which sometimes include product photographs and videos created by the reviewers), Amazon has deepened and broadened its ecosystem in a variety of ways. It created Wish Lists, which enable customers to share their favorite products with others, customer discussion areas to talk about particular products, and general discussion forums for broader topics, including religion, TV series, politics, classic rock, and romance.

As Amazon, Salesforce, Airbnb, and others like them so clearly demonstrate, business ecosystems can be a remarkably powerful driver of revenues and growth, and it's no surprise that many of the most successful companies being created now are ecosystem companies. There are a couple of reasons for this: First, connectivity is so much better than it used to be that it's much easier to build an ecosystem. In fact, you can have a worldwide ecosystem at any level of scale you want. Second, consumers, and increasingly, business buyers, expect to be able to interact with each other.

If you were, for example, a fanatical antique wooden boat refurbisher, you could build an ecosystem of antique wooden boat owners, companies that supply parts for antique wooden boats, people who like to do marketing shoots on antique wooden boats, and organizations that like to sponsor wooden boat gatherings and competitions. You could potentially build an ecosystem around anything that you're interested in. For any product your company is offering, you should ask yourself, "Are we building an ecosystem around this?" and "Do we already have one that we haven't fully nurtured?"

Many very large, long-established companies have noticed the ascendance of business ecosystems, and are establishing their own ecosystems. GE, for example, realized that focusing only on manufacturing and selling equipment would constrain its future growth. The company therefore took steps to build its own ecosystem by creating Predix, a cloud-based "Platform as a Service" (PaaS) that combines analytics with streams of data from industrial sensors, to extend the life of airplane engines, gas turbines, and other equipment, while optimizing their performance.

The Predix Industrial Internet ecosystem includes partners such as AT&T to help develop a secure wireless service; Cisco to build intelligent networking between equipment; Accenture, which was brought in by GE to create analytics apps; and many others. Says Dave Bartlett, chief technology officer for Current, powered by GE, "A software platform becomes more powerful the more people use it. GE will continue using it, but making it available externally will also allow our customers and business partners to write their own software and become more successful. We want Predix to become the Android or iOS of the machine world. We want it to become the language of the Industrial Internet."[13]

GE also realized that it needed its employees to mix with people from other innovative companies to stimulate learning and innovation. In 2016, the company announced that it would move its headquarters from Fairfield, Connecticut, to Boston, Massachusetts. According to former chairman and CEO Jeff Immelt, the move was precipitated by a desire to expand GE's ecosystem and attract the right talent. Immelt pointed out that Boston is an ecosystem made by and for innovation. "In Boston," he said, "we can be challenged by a doctor from Massachusetts General or by a student from MIT. We need to be in this environment."[14]

In the future, businesses will leverage their ecosystems and communities in new ways that haven't even been thought of yet. Airbnb, for example, has an extensive and well-established ecosystem of property owners and guests who have shared needs and interests. What else could this company do with its ecosystem?

The answer to that question is Airbnb Experiences, which was publicly announced in November 2016. This new product offering provides Airbnb customers an opportunity to "learn from local legends, like surf pros, up-and-coming artists, master chefs, and nonprofit founders."[15] So, for example, when I visit San Francisco for business, I can use the Airbnb app to book experiences—anything from a crash course in clowning and juggling, to a hands-on course in food styling and photography, to a three-day session on making the jump into entrepreneurship. According to the company, 10 percent of its experiences will be focused on "social impact," with proceeds going to local nonprofits.[16] If you have a skill or special interest and would like to share it, Airbnb Experiences is there to help you market your services. Similarly, if you want to experience something new, Airbnb can help you find someone to guide your experience.

A Tale of Two Companies

Walmart is the number-one business on the Fortune 500 with annual revenues of $482 billion. The company has 2.3 million employees worldwide, and Walmart is the largest employer in the United States as well as the nation's largest grocer.

Amazon is currently ranked #18 on the Fortune 500, with annual revenues of $107 billion, about one-fifth of Walmart. The company, which jumped to its current position on the Fortune 500 from #29 the year before, has approximately 231,000 employees, or about 10 percent of Walmart's headcount.

One of these companies, Amazon, has built an extensive business ecosystem around its customers, whereas Walmart has not—yet. But make no mistake: Walmart is making tremendous strides in that direction. In fact, after Amazon, Walmart is the second-largest digital retailer in the world, with $13 billion in online sales in 2015. As Walmart continues to build and refine its own ecosystem of brick-and-mortar stores, it is also looking for ways to strengthen its customer ecosystem.

Let's say you want to buy a Spalding NBA street basketball. If you check the item on Amazon, you'll find that it has 2,590 customer reviews and 50 answered questions. In addition, Amazon shows you what items are most often purchased along with the basketball (in this case a Franklin sports ball maintenance kit and a Wilson traditional soccer ball), a variety of videos related to the product (for example, how to do a speed dribble and how to dunk a basketball with one hand), customer photos, a list of other products customers who viewed the Spalding basketball also looked at, and more. The price is $12.99 for the official size version.

If you check the same item on Walmart, you'll quickly notice that there are only 86 customer reviews, just 3 percent of the number of reviews on Amazon, and only four answered questions. Walmart also shows other products customers bought along with the Spalding basketball, and other items they viewed. However, there are no user photos or videos, nor any videos related to the product. Overall, it's clear that there is not much of a customer ecosystem built into Walmart's online experience. And the price is $16.99 for the official size version, four dollars more than the same ball on Amazon.

Although Walmart's customer ecosystem has a long way to go before it can match the one Amazon has built over the years, the company has a very well-established supplier ecosystem, and this supplier ecosystem is a key factor in Walmart's success. In 1992, Walmart rolled out an automated system to its vendors known as Retail Link. The system was designed to strengthen its supplier partnerships; it enables vendors to retrieve a variety of data about how their products are doing in individual Walmart stores, including sell-through data, on-hand inventory by SKU, gross margin achieved, inventory turns, in-stock percentage, and more. This system provides a wealth of data to help suppliers improve their service to Walmart while improving their own financial results. Retail Link allows Walmart to minimize on-hand inventory while at the same time avoiding stock outs, which frustrate customers and result in lost sales for both suppliers and Walmart.

Walmart's Retail Link system has generated its own ecosystem of companies that provide consulting services to Walmart vendors. Enhanced Retail Solutions, for example, provides Retail Link consulting ("We help you keep in stock and create recaps that can easily be turned into actionable scripts or recommendations"[17]), 8th & Walton provides Retail Link live training and webinars (and counts among its clients Johnson & Johnson, Tyson, Goodyear, Kraft, and Procter & Gamble), and there are currently 10 Retail Link expert freelancers available on Upwork.com.

@WalmartLabs, located in the middle of the Silicon Valley in Sunnyvale, California, bills itself as "the idea incubator for the world's largest global retailer."[18] The organization is charged with designing, prototyping, and building technology-fueled products for Walmart that "bridge the gap between what's next and what's best."[19] Recent development projects include a Search My Store feature on the Walmart smartphone app that enables customers to search for products in-store or online, and a pharmacy link, which allows customers to manage and refill prescriptions with their mobile device.

In addition, @WalmartLabs created a baby registry for the Walmart mobile app that users can share with family and friends. Users can select products for their registry on Walmart.com, or they can use their smartphone to scan a product barcode in a Walmart store. The registry is automatically updated when purchasers scan their receipts using the app so parents don't receive duplicate gifts. Walmart appears to be investing its efforts in developing a customer ecosystem that may someday give Amazon a run for its money.

I believe that *any* business can benefit from developing its ecosystem to embrace and encompass its customers, suppliers, and other stakeholders. As predicted by the network effect, the more customers who participate in the network, the more valuable it becomes to customers. Ecosystems can create a virtuous cycle that increases the value a company provides to its customers, enhances customer loyalty, and drives company profits and growth. For those reasons alone, company leaders should ask themselves what role an ecosystem might play in their company's success.

Steps to Creating, Re-creating, or Building a Powerful Ecosystem

As a consultant, I have worked to create my own business ecosystem in the form of a network of Setili & Associates' clients and other business leaders. I created the Strategic Agility Think Tank to explore how organizations can become more strategically agile, and to bring executives together to share ideas and learn from their peers. We host events designed to build connections among corporate peers—CEOs, division presidents, CFOs, CMOs, COOs, and SVPs of sales, marketing, operations and strategy—so that they might learn from one another while strengthening their companies and personal performances.

The Strategic Agility Think Tank connected my community, so that members could build relationships with one another, and help one another solve business problems. It's an ecosystem of people with common areas of interest. This is just one example of how even a small business can create an ecosystem that is incredibly powerful.

Since I started the Strategic Agility Think Tank, more than 70 companies have participated, including AT&T, Delta Air Lines, IBM, Georgia-Pacific, Hilton, SAP, Time Warner, and UPS, representing many billions of dollars of revenue. As a result of this business ecosystem, participants have shared—and received—lots of ideas from one another and have grown their businesses.

If you are in business, you already have an ecosystem. That ecosystem, however, may be holding you back. Figure 5.1 lays out the steps needed to build a more powerful and vibrant ecosystem that can become a self-sustaining driver of your company's growth; the chart at the bottom of this page goes into more detail and expands on those initial steps.

Step 1: Identify who is already in your ecosystem. Some members of your ecosystem may be obvious to you, such as customers whom you talk to frequently, or suppliers who come to your annual conferences. Other ecosystem members may be less obvious. One company I know did not realize that there were developers who specialized in adapting the company's software to niche industries. These developers were flying under the radar, until someone took a close look at who connected to, benefiting from, or doing business with the company.

Step 2: Determine who the ideal members are. You want people and organizations to join your ecosystem whose goals are compatible with yours, and who can help you reach your own goals.

Figure 5.1:

Building a More Powerful and Vibrant Ecosystem

Who is currently in our ecosystem?	Who would we ideally like to have in our ecosystem?	What value will they get, and what will they give?	How can we make it easy for them to interact and gain value?
• Customers • Potential customers • Suppliers • Developers • Franchisees • Distributors, sales agents, retailers, and other channel partners • Installers, technicians, systems integrators, healthcare providers, and other delivery or service partners • Insurers, attorneys, and other ancillary services • Technology partners, researchers • Reviewers and other content creators • Lenders, borrowers • Owners, renters	**Keep, grow, or attract:** • Existing ecosystem members • New ecosystem members **Discontinue or deemphasize:** • Unprofitable customers • Undesirable ecosystem members (such as those who are costly, fraudulent, or inconsistent with your brand and vision)	• Revenues • Knowledge • Relationships • Prestige • Fun • Products • Services • Decisions and approvals • Data • Assets • Technologies	• Platforms • Events • Standard operating procedures, guidelines, templates, and other tools • Directories • Referrals • Reviews, ratings, and recommendations • Payment and escrow systems

Developing clear criteria for who your ideal members are will guide your outreach efforts, and will make the process of growing your ecosystem more efficient and effective. For example, if you're trying to build a community of app developers, you want to attract the best of the best, with a particular set of skills. To attract these developers, you may wish to hold a hackathon or a contest. You may also decide to tailor your market messaging and the design of your platforms to appeal to the particular type of developers you seek to attract.

There also may be members of your ecosystem who will *not* play a role in your ideal future. For example, you may foresee that as you sell more of your products and services direct to consumers via e-commerce and other means, your current distributors and retailers may be bypassed, or become less important. Planning for this likely outcome is crucial.

Other types of ecosystem members who may not be part of your ideal future include unprofitable customer segments, channel partners who deliver a bad customer experience, and fraudulent players. Develop a plan for how to migrate away from these less-desirable ecosystem members.

Step 3: Determine how you would like members to derive and contribute value. People and organizations who participate in ecosystems do so because they derive value from participating. There are myriad forms of value, including making money, gaining referrals and relationships, learning, showing off your skills, and gaining access to information, suppliers, and customers. Ecosystem members also *contribute* value. Some members pay and some members make money—and some members both pay *and* make money, depending on the situation. Some members contribute knowledge, endorsements, reviews, products, time, and the like; others consume these things; and some do both.

You do not always know what is transpiring in your ecosystem, and much of this "give and get" between members may be beyond your control. However, there are some things you can do to positively affect the health, vibrancy, and growth of your ecosystem, and the value derived from it. Here's an example: Among the members of the Amazon ecosystem are self-published authors who make their books available through the Amazon Kindle Owner's Lending Library and Kindle Unlimited services. In 2015, the company changed the way these authors get paid, compensating them based on how many pages of the authors' books users read. Previously, Amazon paid authors based on the number of times each of their books was borrowed, as long as readers made it through at least 10 percent of the book's pages. This prior system led to a poor reader experience, because it created an incentive for authors to serialize their books by breaking them into multiple short books. Amazon switched to the new payment method to motivate authors to write books that actually get read, and that people actually love, because that is what builds loyalty to Amazon, and strengthens its ecosystem.

Step 4: Create a means for current and prospective ecosystem members to easily interact and gain value. Many of your ecosystem members may already be interacting with each other, but there are things you can do—running events, creating technology platforms, and providing connections and referrals, to name a few—to enhance and stimulate that interaction, and to help ecosystem members both give and get more value. Airbnb has created a platform that makes it easy for owners to safely rent out their homes or rooms, and for guests to find a safe, comfortable, and convenient place to stay. Ride-sharing services Uber and Lyft have created platforms that facilitated the creation of new jobs and new forms of transportation. And Setili & Associates has created a way for business leaders to build relationships and learn from each other. Whether high-tech, low-tech, or no-tech, there are things you can do to enhance the value and vibrancy of your ecosystem.[20]

Enhancing Value for Ecosystem Members

The Apple ecosystem creates immense value for its members. Apple cultivates an extensive app developer community, assures that the apps are sound, makes them available through the App Store, enables app developers to make money, and provides its customers with free or low-cost apps that do just about anything you can imagine. Each year, Apple sponsors the Apple Worldwide Developers Conference (WWDC), a multi-day event at which members of the Apple developer community come together "to learn about the future of OS X, iOS, watchOS, and tvOS"—Apple's key operating systems. According to the WWDC site, the event promises "exciting reveals, providing inspiration, and new opportunities to continue creating the most innovative apps in the world."[21]

The Apple App Store is not only a great example of what a vibrant ecosystem can be, but it also shows how an ecosystem can have a powerful financial impact for participants. According to Apple, in 2016 the App Store generated more than $20 billion in revenue for developers and approximately $8.5 billion for Apple itself, due to the portion that Apple earns from each app sold through the App Store. Not only do these apps provide a significant direct boost to Apple's revenue and profit, they also increase the desirability and stickiness of Apple's products, such as iMacs, iPhones, iPads, and the Apple Watch. And Apple reports that 1.4 million new jobs are a direct result of the iOS platform and the App Store.[22] Clearly, the Apple ecosystem creates immense value for the company, for developers, and for Apple users.

Enhancing Value for Your Own Company

Feeding and fortifying your ecosystem can have immense benefits for your own company and can even turn around declining sales. Sales of the popular wearable fitness trackers produced by Fitbit have leveled off in recent years, so the company has begun to invest in cultivating an ecosystem of users. The company's fitness app now includes a community section. This section has a social feed that allows users to post exercise summaries, learn about workouts offered by local fitness trainers, ask and answer questions, and post photos and virtual badges.

The company has not only created virtual ways to interact with other Fitbit users, it has also hosted real-life Fitbit Adventures and Challenges for users to participate in. According to company data, users with one or more friends on the app take an average of 700 more steps a day than those who don't have any friends on the platform.[23]

GoPro, the maker of popular action cameras, faced with a maturing market and declining sales, has invested to build an ecosystem of users. The company encourages GoPro users to upload their videos to YouTube—creating an ecosystem that will increase customer engagement and excite the interest of future customers. To prime the pump, GoPro announced a GoPro Awards program that will award $5 million to users who create unique or interesting content with their GoPros. The program pays out $500 for a winning photo, $1,000 for interesting raw video, and $5,000 for a fully edited video that attracts the company's interest. In doing this, GoPro is capitalizing and building on an ecosystem that had begun to take shape even without company involvement.

Says Zander Lurie, GoPro vice president of media, "We have 15,000 videos uploaded to YouTube each day that are tagged or titled GoPro. We don't ask consumers to do that; they just do it. What we're trying to do is grow our brand and reward community members who are doing cool things with our cameras."[24]

Mistakes to Avoid

Although today's network companies with large ecosystems, such as Uber and Airbnb, make building a powerful platform look easy, creating a growing, sustainable ecosystem is not necessarily an easy thing. Once an ecosystem is established, there's no guarantee that it will keep growing, and customers, suppliers, developers, reviewers, content providers, and other stakeholders may move to more attractive offerings. In an article in *Harvard Business Review*, Marshall Van Alstyne, Geoffrey Parker, and Sangeet Paul Choudary pointed out six reasons why platforms, and the ecosystems they support, may fail.[25]

1. **Failure to optimize "openness."** Having too much or too little control over your platform can both be bad outcomes. If there's too much control, people will feel constrained and unwelcome, and they will seek other, more open platforms. If there's too little control, the company can lose control of its product.

2. **Failure to engage developers.** If developers are an important part of the ecosystem you are cultivating, or one that you envision, you must create a platform compelling enough to attract developers' attention and engagement, and you must support and nurture it. According to the authors, "Successful platforms engage in platform evangelism, providing developers with resources to innovate, feedback on design and performance, and rewards for participating."[26]

3. **Failure to share the surplus.** Everyone who participates in the platform must receive value from their participation. If they don't, then you can't expect them to stick around. Although Amazon profits from the participation of its army of free product reviewers, for example, it provides value to them through Vine—its invitation-only program that rewards its best reviewers with free (often pre-launch) products to review—and by providing recognition to its top reviewers in a variety of different ways on Amazon.com.

4. **Failure to launch the right side.** When you're a company building an ecosystem, and a platform on which to host it, you've got to decide which category of members is most important to grow first to attract the others. For example, suppliers and developers may not join your ecosystem unless there is a critical mass of customers. On the other hand, customers may not join until there is a critical mass of suppliers, or an enticing set of apps. Making the wrong choice about who to attract first may result in the failure of your platform.

5. **Failure to put critical mass ahead of money.** Before you start trying to make money from your platform, you first need to attract a large enough group of people or organizations to sustain and grow it over the long run. If you begin focusing on profits too soon, investing too little in attracting a critical mass of people and organizations, you may set up your platform for irrelevance and failure. Facebook, now extremely successful, invested $2.4 billion to grow its user base before beginning to make money.

6. **Failure of imagination.** Companies that focus only on building and selling products put themselves at a tremendous disadvantage against companies that also create platforms and ecosystems for developers, customers, and others. Building a platform that can grow and thrive over a long period of time requires great imagination on the part of those who are tasked to design it. The more freedom they are given to dream big dreams and then pursue them, the better the chances that they will create a great platform.

As in any other human endeavor, there's the possibility that bad actors are going to gain access to your ecosystem and try to bend it to their own personal advantage, or break it altogether. I used FlipKey, a vacation rental service owned by TripAdvisor, to rent a cottage in Key West. Once I paid my deposit, the "owner" sent me a nice note saying, "Thank you for booking my cottage. I'm sure you'll have a wonderful stay. Please do get in touch if you have any questions about your vacation." I booked plane tickets for our family of four, and looked forward to the rest and relaxation we would enjoy in her cozy cottage. A few weeks later, I received an email from FlipKey saying, "Unfortunately, we had to cancel your rental."

When I called FlipKey, they informed me that the owner who had taken my deposit was fraudulent. The cottage existed; however, it didn't belong to the person who claimed she owned it. In fact, the same cottage now appeared on FlipKey, listed by a *different* owner. Unfortunately for me and anyone else who was a victim of this fraud, FlipKey didn't do a good job keeping bad actors out of their ecosystem. As my trip was fast approaching, we were left with no place to stay. After a time-consuming search online, I found another property that could accommodate our entire family at a premium price because we were booking at the last minute. Debacles like this quickly erode customer trust.

When you create an ecosystem and a platform, you've got to be sure that the system holds people accountable for what they promise. You have to be able to verify that someone is who they say they are while protecting their identity, as appropriate.

When newspapers made the move to the internet, creating online versions of their articles, they enabled people to leave comments after the articles, often creating their own fake names. This, however, sometimes spawned a culture in which people hiding behind a wall of anonymity could leave incendiary comments and insult others in the community, causing them to respond with their own equally aggressive comments, or simply withdraw. To combat this trend, many newspapers now require commenters to sign in using their Facebook accounts and real names. The newspapers found that taking this step made people more accountable in their postings, and reduced the problems created by bad actors.

Some media organizations, including the website for National Public Radio (NPR), have decided to banish comments altogether. According to NPR statistics, in July 2016, the npr.org website had approximately 33 million unique users and 491,000 comments. However, those comments were written by only 0.06 percent of the site's unique users, a very small portion of the overall NPR audience ecosystem. Ultimately, these comments, combined with the relatively high cost of maintaining the system and paying moderators to ferret out and delete inappropriate comments, led NPR to pull the plug on the comment system.[27]

Once you build an ecosystem, or a platform on which to host it, you can't just leave it on autopilot. An ecosystem requires constant attention and nurturing to ensure it will grow while meeting the needs of your company. If it fails to achieve the goals you have set out for creating it in the first place, then you must make the necessary corrections, or pull the plug before it damages your brand.

In Conclusion

Ecosystems can create tremendous value for the businesses that create them, as well as for participants, including customers, suppliers, vendors, and other stakeholders. As you consider creating or growing your own business ecosystem, keep the following points in mind:

- **Create a vision for how your ecosystem can fuel growth.** Companies like Salesforce have created remarkable value for themselves and for their customers, vendors, and others by creating vibrant and growing ecosystems. Regardless of what business or industry you're in, you can create an ecosystem that enables fearless growth as ecosystem members drive value for you and for one another.

- **Determine who is already in your ecosystem, and who you would like to ideally have.** Figure out who is already in your company's ecosystem and whom you would ideally like to have there. Then determine what value you would ideally like each type of ecosystem member to get from the ecosystem, and what value they will provide to you and others within the ecosystem. By being clear on these goals, you can create the platforms, systems, and outreach to drive the type of participation you want.

- **Create a means for ecosystem members to easily interact and gain value.** Building the strength, size, and participation in your ecosystem can fuel growth, build customer loyalty, and insulate your company from market upsets. Consider creating a technology platform to enable richer interactions between ecosystem members, or augment the platform you already have. Facilitate and nurture real-life relationships between ecosystem members, as Salesforce does, through gatherings, conference calls, and introductions.

- **Provide value to members of your ecosystem.** The members of your ecosystem must perceive value from their participation; otherwise, they won't bother to remain a part of it. Be sure that you know what the people and companies that are a part of your ecosystem value, and then provide it.

- **Beware of potential ecosystem killers.** There are a number of things that can undermine or even destroy an ecosystem. Become aware of these potential pitfalls, and then do everything you can to ensure they don't take root in your own ecosystem.

Rule #5: Open the Floodgates of Employee Creativity

In 2000, Google introduced AdWords, a product that served advertisements next to Google search results. Within a couple of years, however, Google cofounder Larry Page was becoming increasingly frustrated with the kinds of ads that were being displayed, as many were completely unrelated to search results. One day he printed out a bunch of the ads, wrote "THESE ADS STINK" across the top, and posted them on a bulletin board before taking off for the weekend.

Someone spotted Page's note, and five engineers started working on a solution to the problem. No one asked the engineers to take on this task, and the engineers were not a part of the company's advertising team. However, they felt challenged to solve the problem, and during that weekend, they came up with a new approach. Instead of serving ads based on which advertiser was willing to spend the most money or which ad received the most clicks, the team created an "ad relevance score" to determine which ads would be presented to each user.

The new approach was better for Google users, and better for advertisers. Today, advertising accounts for just more than 90 percent of the company's annual revenues of $74.5 billion, earning a healthy 25 percent net income.[1]

In their book, *How Google Works*, authors Eric Schmidt, Google's executive chairman and ex-CEO, and Jonathan Rosenberg, former Google SVP of products, say that any company that hopes to achieve success in the Internet Century must attract a new kind of animal: *smart creatives*. According to Schmidt and Rosenberg, smart creatives are analytically smart, business smart, competitive smart, and user smart. A smart creative is "always questioning, never satisfied with the status quo, seeing problems to solve everywhere and thinking that she is just the person to solve them."[2]

According to Schmidt and Rosenberg:

> A smart creative is a firehose of new ideas that are genuinely new. Her perspective is different from yours or ours. It's even occasionally different from her own perspective, for a smart creative can play the perspective chameleon when she needs to . . . Their common characteristic is that they work hard and are willing to question the status quo and attack things differently. This is why they can have such an impact.[3]

Smart creatives take action when they see a problem: They don't wait for someone else to come along and solve it. Engaging employees' creativity is one of the most powerful ways companies, both large and small, can innovate and move quickly.

When employees are fully engaged in their jobs, they give the best of themselves. They provide their employers with new ways of doing things better and faster, while maximizing value for customers. They act fast to get things done. A company with a fully engaged workforce can grow fearlessly because every employee has the company's best interests in mind. Every employee is alert to changes in the marketplace, potential threats, and new opportunities for growth.

There's just one problem: According to Gallup's most recent survey, only 33 percent of U.S. employees are engaged in their jobs. That leaves 67 percent not engaged at work.[4] This is a tremendous problem for businesses in every industry as these millions of unengaged men and women are a vast, untapped source of creativity, innovation, and speed.

So, what is the roadblock—the immovable object—that stands in the way of employee creativity and speed? In many organizations, that roadblock is the organization's leaders.

The good news is that great leadership doesn't have to be hard if leaders simply step back from trying to solve every problem themselves, and instead tap into the brains, hearts, and creativity of their employees. They can accomplish this by communicating a clear purpose and values, asking employees to identify and implement solutions, allowing new ways to work, removing roadblocks to innovation, and ensuring employees get fast feedback on the results of their efforts.

In this chapter, I explore what every leader can do to open the floodgates of employee creativity in their companies, rather than creating an obstacle to employee contributions.

The Power of Delegation

To grow fearlessly and to thrive and succeed in today's environment of fast change, we need to be very adaptable. We need to spot changes in the market as they emerge. We need to come up with smart and differentiated ways of capitalizing on these changes. And we need to take action immediately—not only to serve new customer needs as they emerge, but to anticipate what customers will want years in the future.

To achieve adaptability and agility in our businesses, we need creative, adaptable employees who have the ability to quickly respond to the changes they see around them. We need every employee to be watching, thinking, and taking action.

Figure 6.1 builds on a framework I first introduced in my previous book, *The Agility Advantage.* The figure shows examples of what you would like your employees to be thinking in order to achieve the three elements of business agility: Market Agility, Decision Agility, and Execution Agility.

Adaptability and creativity are closely intertwined; you can't have adaptability without the drive of creative thought. Years ago, I decided to make a cover for our Hobie Cat sailboat to prevent falling leaves from staining the hull. As it turned out, the most important thing was simply to start—to get some material and lay it on top of

Figure 6.1:

The Three Elements of Business Agility

Market Agility	Decision Agility	Execution Agility
Identify potential opportunities that are being created by market change	**Generate creative alternatives for capitalizing on these opportunities, and make fast, fact-based decisions about which alternatives to pursue**	**Enlist and inspire your organization to execute the new direction, and adjust course as events unfold**
To attain Market Agility, your employees should be thinking:	To attain Decision Agility, your employees should be thinking:	To attain Execution Agility, your employees should be thinking:
• "What new customer behaviors and needs do I see?" • "What's new in the competitive environment?" • "How might we improve our processes and tools to increase speed and efficiency?" • "What might we stop doing?"	• "I know what I can decide and what I can take action on." • "When I have a good idea, I know how to get the resources and support I need to bring it to fruition." • "I have a strong network of coworkers who collaborate with me." • "Other decision-makers seek my input."	• "I understand the 'big picture' of what my organization is trying to accomplish." • "I am encouraged to suggest changes, and try new things." • "I enjoy working with my coworkers, customers, and leaders." • "My efforts are recognized, even when progress is slow."

the boat and assess what needed to be done. I asked myself, "What doesn't look right?" The answers became evident: "Oh, here's a place that's going to blow open during a storm. I'll sew strings on each side to tie this down. Here's a wrinkle where the water is going to puddle. I'll put a seam here, then pull the sides down with bungees, to make a roof that can shed the water."

You start, you see what you need—and you adapt from there.

In previous years, corporate leaders were expected to make all the key decisions, leaving employees to merely execute. One of the problems with this top-down approach to decision-making is that anyone who is not at the top feels little responsibility for what happens in their piece of the organization. They play it safe. They keep their heads low, and do what they can to avoid missteps and controversy. In this environment, there's little incentive to come up with new ideas, and considerable risk if you do.

On the other hand, if you want to fuel employee creativity in your organization, try simply being curious and seeking out employee ideas. In his autobiography, *The Virgin Way*, Sir Richard Branson says that seven little words constitute one of the most powerful sentences a business leader can utter: "I'm not sure—what do you think?" Branson continues:

> When a leader displays the self-confidence to effectively say, "Hey, I can't be expected to have all the answers, so I'd love to hear your thoughts on the subject," it not only has a very humanizing effect, but it also tells the employees that their opinions are respected and considered to be of value . . . if your people know that their opinions may be sought at any moment they will pay much closer attention and also have to have an opinion at the ready.[5]

Branson invites people at every level of his businesses to be involved in decisions. Following a more authoritarian, top-down approach, he says, can lead to all sorts of problems:

Call it the "Don't ask me, I just work here" syndrome if you will, but when there is an authoritarian ruler at the top of the heap, almost every layer beneath them is much less likely to make timely decisions based on their own instincts, preferring instead to push everything "upstairs" and thereby reducing the chances of either getting it wrong and/or overstepping their corporate marks.[6]

Today, few leaders can possibly know enough about every aspect of their business to be able to tell their employees what to do in every circumstance. The world changes too quickly, and business today is too complex and global. Every once in a while, there may be an exception to this rule—say, for example, someone like Steve Jobs, whose leadership style was autocratic, and who involved himself in many details of Apple and its products. But these people are few and far between, and most leaders need to hire great people, then delegate as much authority and responsibility to them as they can—unleashing the creativity of every employee. As Branson says, "Nobody can be successful alone—and you cannot be a great leader without great people to lead."[7]

So, what kind of employee are we looking for? Who is most likely to apply their creativity to the work they do? Almost anyone. When people realize that you're going to ask their opinion, they put more thought into their work. They're more collaborative and entrepreneurial. When their leaders look to them for advice and solutions, they become more engaged in their work. When leaders create a system that engages the minds of their people, employees will always be thinking about how the company can advance its top priorities. When leaders reveal their ignorance, employees will share their knowledge and ideas.

If you want your organization to grow fearlessly and to be agile and adaptable, you've got to get everyone involved thinking about your problem or your objective. In a post on LinkedIn, GE's former chairman and CEO Jeff Immelt explained that although GE is a century-old company, it needs to move fast, take risks, fail fast, and act like a startup. Until recently, he said, management could "make every decision at the headquarters." Now, things are different. "We have to embrace decentralization and use technology to help our people to stay connected. . . . We are changing the plumbing inside the company to connect everyone and make the culture change possible. This is existential and we're committed to this."[8]

Engage Employees in the Purpose of Your Business

Lisa Earle McLeod, author of *Leading With Noble Purpose* and other books, defines a business's noble purpose as

> [a] declarative statement about the impact your organization has on customers. But more than a mere message, noble purpose is the lynchpin for a customer-focused strategy that drives competitive differentiation and emotional engagement. Your noble purpose tells the market what you stand for, and why your organization exists.[9]

McLeod cites research that shows organizations with a noble purpose, that focus on improving life for their customers, outperform organizations that are focused on hitting financial targets. Why? Because everyone wants to have a positive impact on the people around them; we all want to change the world for the better. When people know they are working in service to something bigger than themselves—making the lives of their customers and communities better in some way—they will naturally be more engaged and they will naturally give more of themselves to their jobs. Even more important, McLeod says, "Using noble purpose as the driver results in differentiated ideas that actually drive the business."

This may be especially true of the millennial generation, born between 1981 and 2000. According to the 2016 Deloitte Millennial Survey, 87 percent of the millennials surveyed believe that "the success of a business should be measured in terms of more than just its financial performance." In addition, the majority of millennials believe that business has the potential to do good, with 73 percent agreeing that business has a positive impact on wider society.[10]

At her first Noble Purpose Institute, Lisa Earle McLeod gathered a group to explore how to implement a company's noble purpose. That is, what steps are needed to change employee behavior and bring the noble purpose to life? She gave the group an exercise— a case study about an Italian restaurant whose noble purpose was to "bring people together for conversations around the table."[11] She asked the group *not* to focus on how to bring customers into the restaurant, but rather, to come up with ideas on how the restaurant could achieve its purpose of bringing people together.

The group became very inventive. They recommended giving away "conversation cards" to jump-start a fascinating discussion around the kitchen table, or at a dinner party. They suggested posting video clips of funny, awkward, or heartwarming dinner-table conversations on Facebook. They proposed giving kids bread dough that they could use to shape their own rolls at the table (both to stimulate conversations with the kids, and to keep them entertained so the adults could talk). The point is: When the group didn't have to focus on attracting customers to come into the restaurant, but was instead focused on fulfilling the restaurant's noble purpose, they were much more creative. They came up with great marketing ideas by *not* trying to come up with marketing ideas.

Inspire employees with a noble purpose, and you'll be well on the way to building an organization that is fast, adaptable, and agile—a key to surviving and thriving in today's fast-changing markets.

Change the Game

I recently worked with a large, successful company whose growth had slowed. They needed new ideas—and not just any ideas, but *big* ideas: new growth trajectories that would generate at least a billion dollars in revenue. Entirely new categories. They were already one of the largest players in their industry, so taking market share was not easy for them. They needed to build new markets—creating and serving customer needs that had never before existed.

The problem was the ideas just weren't flowing from the team. They had smart people who knew the industry inside and out. They had a large strategy group, but the group was primarily skilled at developing plans to incrementally grow the existing business. Their *modus operandi* was to pass out templates to the business units, then to roll up the plans submitted by the business units into a comprehensive plan for growth.

The growth ideas the company generated in this way tended to always be "more of the same." The managers in the business units may have had great ideas—maybe even phenomenal, world-changing ideas—but they lacked the power or resources needed to accomplish these ideas on their own, so it would have been foolish to submit these grand ideas as part of the strategic planning process. Plus, the growth plans that each business unit submitted tended to get rolled into the coming year's budget, and bonuses depended on bringing in the revenue to meet the budget. Reach too far in the strategic plan, and you'd pay the price later.

As a result, the ideas that business units submitted were low-risk, and close-to-home—things they were confident they could accomplish. Gain a few new customers. Roll out a "new and improved" product. Cross-sell a few new products into existing customer accounts. Gain a little market share. All *great* things to do, but these are the ways you grow just 2 or 3 percent—barely keeping up with the economy—and definitely not the way you grow in a big way, over a sustained period of time.

Sometimes, the smart strategy people at headquarters would come up with a big, world-changing idea. Given their position in the organization, they had the power to marshal the resources needed to bring new ideas to fruition—provided they could justify the investment. They, however, had been trained, through years of experience, to submit very precise numbers, and to be sure the numbers were achievable. They had not, in the past, been rewarded for taking risks. They had seen people who pursued unsuccessful new growth ideas fired or passed over for promotion, and they didn't want that to happen to them. (As my horse wrangler friend once told me, "Your horse is always learning, even if he's not learning what you want him to learn.")

When we encounter a problem like this, as we often do in our consulting work, we need to change the game. The same process that has for years generated 2- to 3-percent growth is not going to generate big, innovative ideas. The following list includes some team exercises you can use to change the game and encourage people to offer their "big" ideas.

- **Play a game.** Frame the exercise as a competition or game: This frees people to take more risk. Try running a *Shark Tank*–style competition.
- **Guess.** Encourage intelligent guessing, and reinforce the fact that excessive precision is inefficient (and creativity-stifling).
- **Change the assumptions.** Encourage teams to challenge the assumptions behind today's ways of doing business. Show how varying those assumptions might affect the outcome. A bank asked: "What if we stopped doing business at our branches, and interacted with customers predominantly through a text messaging app?"

A manufacturing facility asked: "What if we dedicated one set of machines to short runs of customized products and another set of machines to long runs of 'stock' products?" A hotelier asked: "What if we stopped worrying about capacity utilization, and instead focused only on customer satisfaction?"

- **Break through the risks.** When you sense hesitancy to go down a strategic path due to the risks entailed, encourage teams to search for ways to eliminate or mitigate the risks, rather than avoiding high-risk paths altogether.
- **Change the audience.** If, in the past, the team has presented their growth ideas to the senior leadership team, have them instead present to a group of outsiders. Bring in a few venture capitalists or angel investors, or a trusted consultant who can provide an external point of view. Anything you can do to make the exercise "feel" different than your usual strategic planning processes will help spark creative thinking.
- **Involve outsiders.** Pepper the teams with people from the outside. Getting customers, external partners, and people with diverse views involved in generating growth ideas can yield immense benefits. If it's not practical to include people from outside your company, consider including employees from other functions.
- **Cultivate diverse teams.** Research shows that diverse teams are smarter, make better decisions, and are more innovative. In addition, the companies they work for have financial returns above their industry mean.[12] In addition to ethnic, gender, and racial diversity, it's valuable to have a variety of different thinking styles on a team. Include creative people, analytical people,

hands-on people who know the nuts and bolts of how to get things done, and amiable people who are good net-workers and bridge-builders. Diverse mindsets and skill sets on the team make for better results.

In Chapter 6 of my book *The Agility Advantage*, I share many ideas on how to develop breakthrough strategies, and Chapter 7 of the same book shares techniques for managing risk. (Templates and tools from these chapters are available at *www.setili.com/frameworks*.)

Put on Your Competitor's Hat

When we fail to put ourselves in the shoes of our competitors, we tend to overestimate our own company's strengths and competitive position, while underestimating our competitors'. While beating our chests and congratulating ourselves on our competitive prowess, our competitor sneaks up and releases a groundbreaking new product, or steals our best customer.

Spending a couple of days each year in a "war games" exercise can work wonders by forcing people to put themselves in the mindset of the competitor. By knowing the background, personalities, and predispositions of specific leaders in the competitor organization, and playing those roles in a game-like scenario, we can get better insights on what competitors are likely to do next, and how we can respond faster and more capably when they do. Here are some typical outcomes from such exercises:

- One team studied competitors' recent strategic moves, and the experience and background of key leaders. They listened to investor calls to better understand the way competitor leaders thought, and their motivations. They then asked, "What would I do next, if I were them?" As a result, the team identified three customer segments that the competitor was highly unlikely to invest in. They doubled-down on efforts to penetrate these segments, devoting extra sales resources and developing tailored service offerings. They enjoyed the rapid growth that followed.

- Another team realized that their primary competitor had recently brought in a new chief technology officer who had deep experience in e-commerce. Subsequently, when this competitor rolled out a raft of e-commerce enhancements a few months later, with deep discounts for customers who shifted their business to that channel, the team was prepared and suffered minimal market share loss.

- A third team discovered a "hole" in their competitor's product line: The competitor offered no product tailored to the hospitality market. By investing swiftly to serve this underserved market, my client was able to achieve strong growth.

Playing war games enables us to uncover blind spots regarding market realities and competitor capabilities. It enables us to anticipate likely competitor actions, and to plan for potential shifts in the market environment.

Through war games, we can increase the speed and agility with which we can act to accomplish strategic goals, because leaders are aligned and have considered likely competitive scenarios. They will be more prepared to act quickly when the market changes, because they know where each other stand on the issues, and have mentally rehearsed potential responses to competitive scenarios.

People like games. The point is winning, and we can do anything within the rules to win. Game-makers tout that their offerings are "games of skill and chance" because people like both. We like the "skill" part, because it feels good to prove that we have the smarts to beat the competition. We love the "chance" part because even if we fall way behind our opponent halfway through the game, we can always hope that luck will intervene. Playing a war game does wonders for increasing both your skill and luck.

Communicate Clear Values

We need *all* our employees to be constantly thinking, adapting, and creating. Having a clear intent or purpose is crucial for on-the-fly course corrections, innovation, motivation, learning new skills and capabilities, and for getting the entire organization focused on what's important, so they can act as quickly as possible. When you understand your purpose—*why* your company does what it does—and communicate it consistently and often, then employees will get creative about how to achieve it.

Creativity sometimes introduces problems, however. When leaders at Wells Fargo decided that the bank needed to grow market share, they determined that a key lever to do so was to sign customers up for new accounts. So, in a "race to eight," Wells Fargo set an internal goal of selling at least eight financial products to every single customer. According to a lawsuit later filed against the bank, employees who did not meet the sales goals were "reprimanded and told to do whatever it takes to meet individual sales goals."[13]

That "whatever it takes" resulted in the unleashing of a considerable amount of employee creativity, but not the right kind. More than 2.1 million fake deposit and credit-card accounts were created by Wells Fargo employees. The employees found ways to subvert the account sign-up system—setting bogus PINs on debit cards without customer authorization and inputting fake generic email addresses to ensure customers were unaware that accounts were being set up in their name.

Eventually, 5,300 Wells Fargo employees were fired for creating bogus accounts, the bank was fined $185 million by regulators, and CEO John Stumpf was forced to retire.

Wells Fargo's value was "grow market share"—which is not an uncommon one in the world of business. But problems started when the company didn't have the other values, such as honesty and protecting the interests of its customers, which should have gone with it. You want to give your people the freedom to be creative, because this enables you to be big and fast. But, when you give them the freedom to be creative, you also need to impart the right values so that they understand the boundaries of the field on which they are playing.

If employees are not guided by clear values, a few bad apples in your organization may impose their own, and you may end up with the kind of unintended consequences that got Wells Fargo into so much trouble.

Set clear company values and communicate them often. Clear values set the boundaries within which you must operate to achieve your vision. Says Georgia-Pacific's Billy Medof, "At Georgia-Pacific, we think in terms of ten guiding principles. Our fourth one is 'principled entrepreneurship.' These are two words that are important together. This means acting with integrity and a sense of ownership, treating projects as if one were an owner of the company, rather than an employee."[14]

Discover What You Already Know

When you're looking to solve a problem, don't overcomplicate things. Sometimes the simplest solutions are the best.

The treatment of heart attacks represents one of the greatest medical success stories of the past several decades. Although heart disease remains the leading cause of death in the United States as of this writing—with almost one death every minute from heart attacks and coronary artery disease—the death rate fell by 38 percent from 2003 to 2013.[15] And although healthier diets, lower smoking rates, and improved drugs and medical treatments all played a role in this decline, faster emergency treatment was a key reason.

Hospitals across the country have dramatically reduced "door-to-balloon" time—the time from when a patient enters the hospital to when doctors clear the blockages in the patient's arteries to get blood flowing to the heart again. But what's particularly interesting—and instructive—is that this feat has been accomplished with no new medical discoveries, no new technologies, and no new payment incentives. Cardiac teams instead uncovered existing best practices—simple, commonsense solutions thought up by medical personnel across the country—and spread the word about them.

As it turned out, the fastest hospitals weren't the big, famous institutions you would expect to see on such a list; some of the fastest were small town and community hospitals. But they had a few things in common: The best performers had ambulance paramedics transmit electrocardiogram results to the emergency room, so the ER team could prepare. They gave the emergency room doctor power to decide whether the surgery team would be summoned from their beds, rather than having to first consult with cardiologists. They eliminated the need to fill out long consent forms before work got started. And they sounded the beepers for the entire surgery team simultaneously, instead of calling individual team members one by one.

According to the American College of Cardiology, almost every hospital in the United States now treats at least half of their patients in 61 minutes or less.[16]

The development of simple best practices—shared across organizations—can dramatically improve results, yet it often doesn't happen. Business units are heads-down, dealing with their own problems. They don't take the time to learn from other areas of the company. Because different internal groups compete for funding, promotions, and management attention, they sometimes even actively *avoid* sharing their best insights with each other. Even if employees have the best intentions to share their learnings, they have difficulty recognizing best practices in their own units that should be shared with others.

Here are a few tips for spotting—and benefiting from—best practices within your organization:

- **Choose the right metrics.** In comparing hospitals, researchers were wise to choose the "door-to-balloon" metric. It was an easily understood metric that tied directly to what really counted: preventing deaths.
- **Know who is performing well.** This is harder than it seems. For example, the age and health of the population being treated by each hospital greatly affected hospital outcomes. In order to identify the real high-performing hospitals, researchers had to adjust for such factors.
- **Deploy a team.** Ask an unbiased group to compare processes across business units, to find the commonalities, and to communicate what they find. I once worked with a client team to uncover best practices across a large and diverse set of third-party sales agencies. We interviewed, we observed, we analyzed, and we compared. Our objectivity was integral to being able to identify a few key performance drivers, including recruiting and compensation policies, sales approaches, pricing, and operations procedures. Implementing these across the business helped drive a 23-percent increase in margin.
- **Create forums for sharing.** One company I know holds a short conference call every Friday. More than 300 employees participate, although they are not obligated to attend. Three or four people are selected each week to share a technique they used to help a customer or make a sale. The entire call takes only 15 minutes, but

it is immensely valuable in improving performance and motivation.

- **Create a best-practices repository that all business units can access.** When I was a consultant at McKinsey & Company, I could tap into a database of learnings from prior, similar projects whenever I began work in an industry or function I had little experience with. Being able to access—and contribute to—stores of collective knowledge can make even the newest employee far more effective.

- **Identify internal experts on various topics, and make sure employees know how to reach them.** EnPro Industries has done a superlative job at this. It freed up experts' time to answer questions, provide advice to teams, and travel to observe, advise, and learn from business units outside their own. These experts spread ideas between business units and connected employees for collaborative problem-solving.

- **Consider changing power, policy, and process.** To speed up emergency room response time, hospitals had to give emergency room doctors far more power than they previously had. They had to change long-held policies requiring completion of time-consuming consent forms. And they had to change the process—transmitting electrocardiogram results as the ambulance was en route to the hospital. None of these three—power, policy, and process—were easy to change, but they all made an immense difference in improving heart attack outcomes.

- **Focus on the good you are trying to do, rather than competition between business units.** Healthcare workers are highly motivated to save lives, so they worked together to bring down door-to-balloon time nationwide. Your company may not be saving lives, but you're doing something important. Focus on the value you are creating for customers, the great service you provide, or creating an even better place to work. Putting the good you are doing—your noble purpose— at the forefront will stimulate creativity and collaboration across the organization.

Make the Most of Your Newcomers

At Microsoft (which has recently garnered accolades in the media for reemerging as a tech leader after many years playing catch up) CEO Satya Nadella broke longtime company protocol by inviting the heads of companies newly acquired by Microsoft to the company's annual executive retreat. Over the protests of more than a few Microsoft senior leaders—who felt these newcomers didn't have the standing or sufficient experience within the company to make meaningful contributions—Nadella insisted on their presence. Why? Explained Nadella to a Microsoft executive, "We're doing this because of the insights they bring." To move the company forward, Microsoft needs newcomers to challenge the stagnant thinking of longtime employees. Satya proves this assertion by pointing to the company's past failures to set the pace for their industry.[17]

Keep the Senior Team Fresh

Research from Michael Tushman of the Harvard Business School shows that the longer senior management teams are together, the poorer their performance. "The pattern is the same across industries and countries," Tushman says, with the average peak performance occurring when the team has been together around 2.5 years. When a senior team has been in place longer than that, the performance of the entire organization declines. Tushman continues, "It's not that familiarity breeds contempt; that would actually be a good thing if contempt provoked some disagreement and debate. Instead, group members—whether on a board, senior management team, or project team—lose their edge and their ability to deal with conflict, and they begin to think alike."[18]

Leadership teams that have been together too long, in the same roles, talking about the same problems, using the same processes, year after year, become complacent. They have difficulty seeing things any other way than the way they have become accustomed to seeing them. They know each other's preferences and tendencies, and they account for them in their dialog and actions.

If team members have raised issues in the past, and lost the argument, they are unlikely to raise those issues again. One senior leader I know said of his colleague, the president of another division, "Bob has a strong belief that we should continue to invest in his business unit, despite the signs that his market is shrinking and will likely never recover." The leader explained that some of the company's best talent, and the lion's share of IT and capital expenditure budgets, were tied up in his colleague's struggling business, adding, "I think we should redeploy resources to our most attractive growth opportunities, but I'm not going to fight that fight again."

The consequences of groupthink can be devastating when there is an external threat or disruption to the status quo. Senior leadership teams often fail to spot the threat, or fail to respond fast enough. The simplest way to solve this problem is through deliberate succession, or rotating leaders into new roles.

Equifax provides a particularly fitting example. In October 2015, the company rotated the division presidents of each of its four businesses for the second time in five years. Thus, each business had a new leader, with fresh ideas. And each president had a new role, with an opportunity to grow and to address new challenges.

The rotation was just one of many talent development strategies the company uses to maintain a nimble and resilient organization. Each business president was new to his business, but not new to Equifax. It was interesting to watch as the changes took place. Well-established protocols and patterns of reporting, managing, and decision-making were disrupted—in a good way. The company stopped doing a few outdated or no-longer-high-priority things that prior leaders had started. The changes energized the organization by providing new visibility to people in the next layers of management, new points of view on threats to the business, and new vibrancy to growth and innovation initiatives.

Create Mechanisms for Real-Time Feedback to Employees

Adobe, Accenture, GE, Microsoft, and other companies are scrapping annual performance reviews in favor of frequent, real-time feedback focused on continuous improvement. GE created an app called PD@GE (Performance Development at GE), allowing employees to give and request feedback anytime from their manager, peers, or people outside of their business unit. In the app, employees store a list of short-term goals. Managers have frequent discussions with each employee about progress on the goals. Companies found that it's more effective for employees to get up-to-the-minute insights from their colleagues about what they can do better, rather than annual feedback from the boss, when neither party might remember much about what happened months ago.[19]

In my book *The Agility Advantage,* I cited the example of Harvard Business School professor Teresa Amabile, who analyzed 12,000 diary entries of employees from a variety of industries. She found that 76 percent of people reported that their best days involved making progress toward goals. The best way for employees to know that they have made progress in their work, she explains, is to get feedback from the work itself. "The key, then, is to design each job so that, in the act of carrying out the work, people gain the knowledge about the results of their effort."[20] This can be as simple as encouraging employees to comment on what the group has accomplished at the end of each meeting.

Eliminate the Silo Effect

Functional silos can turn decision-making into an excruciatingly slow process. To grow fearlessly, we want to empower employees to take action without asking permission or getting approvals. However, empowering employees gets trickier when more than one silo is involved. A "silo effect" occurs when an employee in Silo A sees an opportunity that cannot be solved within her own silo. She may have to convince her boss, or boss's boss, to talk to the leader of Silo B, who then has to pass the message down the chain to the responsible group in Silo B. It gets complicated and, needless to say, slow.

If we can better integrate across silos we can grow faster. The problem is that this is often very complex and counter-cultural in an organization that has operated for years in a silo structure.

To alleviate the silo effect, establish common goals that span silos. For example, Delta Air Lines has set a goal of winning the top J.D. Power customer satisfaction ranking for airlines. Every unit of the company contributes to this goal. Mechanics assure that the planes are reliable, the technology group assures that the website and app work perfectly, the flight crews provide great onboard service, and the gate and ground crews ensure passengers have a great experience in the airport and that their luggage is well cared for. Even staff functions like finance and legal find ways to contribute.

Perhaps the most powerful lever for fostering cross-silo collaboration is to establish teams focused on solving a particular problem or realizing a particular opportunity. McKinsey authors John Dowdy and Kirk Rieckhoff report that firms such as Google, ING, and Siemens have achieved greater organizational agility by setting up modular, cross-silo teams that "have clear missions with autonomy to make decisions and are charged with end-to-end ownership of a process with a clear customer."[21]

One company I know has a group focused on the customer journey. This group looks at the customer experience across every touchpoint. The group identifies those points in the customer journey that are the biggest pain points for the customer, and the biggest opportunities for the company to improve the experience to gain sales and customer loyalty. When they identify a specific problem or opportunity, they form a team comprised of representatives of each "silo" to fix it. Teams work together to address these opportunities, then disband when the opportunity is achieved. An important side benefit is that team members get to know employees who work in functions and business units other than their own. These informal, silo-bridging relationships create a network that is valuable to both the individuals and the company as a whole.

Allow New Ways to Work

Companies are experimenting with all sorts of new ways to work—ways that are much more akin to new-economy companies like Uber than they are the legacy companies that have been around and stuck in their ways for decades. One of the great things about Uber is that drivers can work when and where they want to. They can turn on the app anytime they want, and then turn the app off and stop working when they decide. They can even set a preference for their last trip of the day to terminate near home. So, for example, they can slip 45 minutes of Uber work in between their primary job and picking up their child at school.

So, why not allow an engineer to design a valve in a similar way? Pay the employee to design the valve; don't pay them for the hours they work. Let *them* decide when and where they'll work, so long as they meet required deadlines. Employees would certainly appreciate this approach. A 2014 Citigroup and LinkedIn survey found that nearly half of employees would give up a 20-percent raise for greater control over how they work.[22]

We're all familiar with the standard five-day, 40-hour workweek. Of course, many of us may work even more hours, but most workers are expected to show up at work five days a week, and work eight hours each day. But what if we treated employees more like responsible independent contractors? And what if we paid them by the project, instead of by the hour? And what if we allowed them to work whenever and wherever *they* decided to work?

Although Zappos has attracted no small amount of controversy for its approach to doing business, one thing they do right is creating new ways for employees to work. Zappos employees have no titles and can "opt in" to self-organizing "circles" that are focused on certain projects and programs. Each employee can choose up to 10 different circles, pursuing what interests him or her most. Not only can they select the projects they most want to work on, they can choose the role they want to play on each project. An employee's role can be different from project to project. If you're primarily a marketing professional, for example, but you think you might really enjoy project management, you could choose to be a project manager on one of the projects. On another project, you could play a technical role, or a facilitator role.

Circles form and disband spontaneously when their purpose is completed. Rather than keeping track of titles and reporting relationships, as most companies do, Zappos uses software (GlassFrog, from the Holacracy company) to keep track of which circles each employee is in, and what each circle has accomplished and decided.

When you can create mechanisms that enable people to work in ways that suit their own personal style and interests, it's good for the employee, for the organization, and, ultimately, for the customer. Employees gain new tools, knowledge, and confidence by gaining experience with different roles, different kinds of work, and different kinds of projects. They become more creative and effective, and more expansive in their thinking.

Some of the new, online collaboration work tools such as Slack and Asana can help people connect with other like-minded people throughout their organizations to work on common issues. When you find someone in another business unit, or another country, who has the same problem as you, it can reinvigorate your problem-solving energy and ingenuity. Employees can contribute in new ways, and get feedback from the work itself through these tools.

Allowing new ways of working doesn't mean that you must upend your current organizational structure, or adopt radically new policies and practices. For a large, established company like Delta Cargo, the logistics arm of Delta Air Lines, it can simply mean instilling a culture that is more entrepreneurial. Gareth Joyce, president of Delta Cargo, wants to make Delta Cargo an entrepreneur inside Delta, a nimble business that can move faster, and "cut through the jungle a little quicker" than Delta as a whole. To accomplish this goal, Joyce knows that he needs the engaged creativity of Delta Cargo's employees—their suggestions and good ideas—from every level of the organization, and in every part of it. "If we can make our business one where we're thought-starters, a little more curious, more willing to take risks like a company in Silicon Valley," Joyce adds, "then we can be a seed environment for human capital."[23]

And, ultimately, that's what it comes down to: human capital. People.

When you unleash the creativity of your people, remarkable things can happen. When asked what his leadership style is, Joyce begins by saying, "I ask a lot of questions and listen."[24] Take a moment to step back and assess your own leadership style. Are your employees engaged in their work, or are they just going through the motions? If it's the latter, what are you and your leadership team doing to stand in the way of their engagement—and creativity?

The sooner you figure out the answers to these questions, and take steps to change the status quo, the sooner the full potential of your organization will be unleashed.

In Conclusion

Your employees are a deep and wide ocean of creative knowledge. You'll never know how much they can offer to your organization and your customers if you don't get them involved and engaged in every aspect of your business. As you consider unleashing the creativity of your employees, be sure to keep the following points in mind:

- **Delegate, empower, and admit ignorance.** Push decision-making down to the lowest practical levels. Reveal your own ignorance so people at all levels feel welcome to share their opinions and perspectives.
- **Engage employees in your purpose.** People, especially millennials, want to have a positive impact on the world. Inspire your employees with a sense of purpose, and they will be more creative and energized.
- **Change the game.** Using the same processes over and over can lull people to sleep. To spur employee energy and creativity, try changing the assumptions, posing new questions, or introducing a competition or game designed to achieve business goals. Games stimulate new ways of thinking, and free people to take more risk.

- **Put on your competitor's hat.** Study your competitors' recent moves and what their leaders are doing and saying. Anticipate what competitors may do next, and how you might respond. Seek out the areas competitors are neglecting, and focus on serving those markets.
- **Communicate clear values.** Growing fearlessly requires empowering employees to work more autonomously, but clear values are required to assure that they do the right things when confronted with new challenges. Communicate your values clearly and frequently, so that employees know what you expect, even when no one is looking.
- **Discover what you already know.** Sometimes simple solutions are best. Take the time to identify and share best practices between different areas of your company.
- **Make the most of your newcomers.** People who are new to your organization can bring new insights and break up patterns of stagnation. Give them broad exposure to others in the organization.
- **Allow new ways to work.** Flexibility in when and where people work can increase employee satisfaction, productivity, and creativity. Consider project-based groups, rather than top-down structures. Encourage collaboration across units to solve problems.

Rule #6: Achieve Fast and Fearless Learning

"Building a company is like following the scientific method," says Facebook founder and CEO Mark Zuckerberg. "You try a bunch of different hypotheses."[1] His approach has served the company well. Facebook is the sixth-most-valuable public company in the world, and its annual growth rate has been an impressive 50 percent for the past four years.

Unlike some companies that grow fast and become huge, but fail to achieve high profits, Facebook is remarkably profitable. In 2016, the company earned $7 billion in profit on revenue of $27 billion.

Zuckerberg's hacker mentality and the company's constant, massive-scale experimentation have been key drivers behind Facebook's extraordinary trajectory of profitable growth. "He believes in rolling out products quickly: 'Move fast and break things' is a company motto."[2] The company runs tens of thousands of different versions of its site at any given time. You may see a version of an ad with one set of colors and features, whereas I see another—simultaneously. Facebook engineers measure customer response, retaining the versions that perform the best and eliminating the others.

The common denominator driving Facebook's success is a constant focus on learning—trying new things all the time, experimenting all the time—and then using the lessons they learn from their experiments to improve what they do in the future. It is this focus on learning that allows Facebook, and many other large companies, to move quickly in the marketplace while always staying a step (or two or three) ahead of their competition.

Achieving Dynamic Stability

Things look good for Facebook now, but at the time of its initial public offering in 2012, the company was in crisis, because a large portion of Facebook users had shifted from using Facebook on their desktop computers to using it on their mobile devices. "We had a problem," chief operating officer and second-in-command, Sheryl Sandberg, explained, "which was that we had exactly no revenue on mobile."[3] The company's ability to adapt very quickly to this change in consumer behavior was extraordinary. Though Facebook was late to the game of mobile advertising, in the four years since the company sold its first mobile ads in 2012, it has grown mobile advertising to 82 percent of total revenue. Facebook's various apps now account for 30 percent of mobile internet use by Americans.

When the world around us is changing fast, as it was for Facebook in 2012, we need to continuously adapt. If we don't adapt quickly in response to changes in customer behavior, technologies, regulations, and other elements of our business environment, we will not only fall behind, but we can also become disoriented and disconnected. We miss market signals. Customers begin to ignore us and look to others for innovation. We fall further and further behind.

The fastest-adapting companies are those that engage in a cycle of experimenting, learning from successes and failures, and applying their new knowledge to the next round of innovation. They grow fearlessly.

Astro Teller, CEO of X, Alphabet's moonshot factory, explains that to increase our rate of learning and improvement, we need to figure out how we can "make the same mistake in half the time and for half the money." Teller suggests that by learning fast, we can achieve *dynamic stability*. I define this as stability created by the act of moving fast. "It's like riding a bicycle," says Teller. "If you stand still, you fall over, but once you're moving it's actually easier. We must learn to exist in this state."[4]

Beware Plateaus

To grow fast and weather the upsets of a fast-changing business environment, we must be in a constant state of change, constantly learning. When we've just been through a period of intense change or innovation, it's tempting to take a breather. Our instinct is to let things settle into a steady state. We reach a plateau of learning, and wish to enjoy the fruits of our labor.

This is dangerous.

"Growth, left alone, will always plateau, and plateaus will always erode,"[5] says Alan Weiss, author of *The Innovation Formula,* who provided the inspiration for Figure 7.1 on page 170. Companies that settle in for a period of stability, a comfortable plateau, will stagnate. Knowledge calcifies. People begin to believe that the status quo is the only logical way to do business. When confronted with ideas for change, they mostly see obstacles. Not only that, but it is also during these plateaus that companies are most exposed to competitors who see their success and set out to replicate it.

When you are stationary, you are a sitting duck, easy to copy and vulnerable to commoditization. You quickly lose your edge.

Figure 7.1:

Avoid Plateaus by Jumping to the Next S-Curve

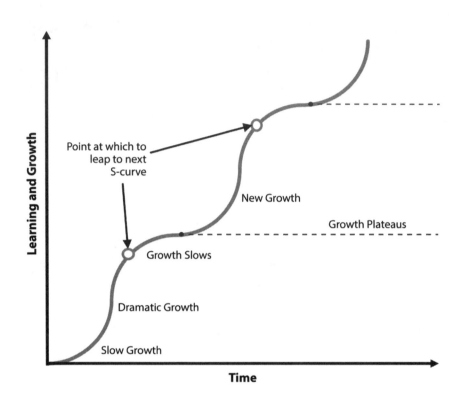

To achieve quantum leaps in capability, we must be willing to disrupt established systems and to try new things. We must extend our vision beyond what we can see today, and we must be willing to adopt a continuous cycle of innovation. We must leap to the next period of rapid learning and innovation—the next S-curve—the moment we have achieved each level of success, rather than allowing ourselves to plateau. It is through this constant experimenting, learning, and innovating that we achieve the dynamic stability that enables speed.

The Value of Fast Learning

Continuous, fast learning can be difficult to maintain, but when you hit your stride and achieve dynamic stability, you will gain great value. The advantages of this type of fast and fearless learning include:

- You will bring new value to your customers more frequently.
- You will "get better at getting better," strengthening the learning muscle throughout your entire organization.
- You will be more prepared for whatever the future might bring, because you will have the skills to adapt. (I love the expression "The more you know, the less you need." If your organization is in the habit of constantly learning, you can surmount any curveball the future throws at you.)
- You will create more differentiated product and service offerings. As a result, competitors will be less able to copy you. You'll be protected from commoditization, and you will enjoy higher margins.
- Because you can adapt fluidly to changes in your business environment, such as changes in customer behavior, technology, and regulations, your offerings will be less likely to become obsolete, outdated, or irrelevant. (BlackBerry, Blockbuster, Kodak, and Nokia all led their industries for years, and have each become irrelevant or shrunk to a small fraction of their former size.)
- You will find and realize new avenues for growth. When entering a new market or offering a new product, sales skills and marketing knowledge are often a bottleneck to growth. In a fast-learning organization, however, sales and marketing break through these barriers fast.

They quickly learn how to sell in the new market or how to describe the benefits of the new product in the customer's words. As a result, you will increase your odds of success and will ramp up revenues faster.

- You will be better able to attract top talent because people who are smart, creative, and courageous want to work for companies that try new things and have a robust outlook for growth.
- Your work will be more fun and rewarding. You'll certainly avoid boredom!
- You will shape your own destiny as a company, and as individuals within that company.

Fast, Fearless Learning Enables a Fluid and Adaptive Strategy

Most great strategies are not arrived at through analysis, market research, and PowerPoint presentations. They are arrived at through trial and error. They are forged through constant experimentation, getting out there and seeing what customers are *really* willing to pay for, what the *real* value is to them, and how strong their loyalty *really* is. No amount of analysis can substitute for constant testing and learning in the real world.

I recently attended a meeting in which the CEO of a global company explained the difficulty of making strategies and plans: "Each year, we develop strategies, and plan to execute them. But then, in the first quarter, five different things happen that are completely inconsistent with what the strategy said. So, we have to go back to the drawing board and think again." That's typical for the world we're in today. We can't plan very far ahead because we don't know what's going to happen tomorrow, much less a year from now. The best thing that we can do is design our strategy in a way that generates learning.

It's a mistake to restrict our aspirations to what we can accomplish with today's capabilities. If we do so, we risk obsolescence. We need to change as fast, or faster, than our customers and competitors to stay relevant.

Too often, companies say, "We haven't been able to do it before, so therefore we can't do it in the future." When a team member suggests ideas for growth and innovation, her colleagues are apt to respond, "We tried that. It didn't work." It can be hard to grow new capabilities and mindsets in a well-established organization. The new capabilities you seek run counter to the established culture that made you successful in the first place.

One organization I worked with sought to improve its marketing prowess, but struggled. "We want to be a marketing powerhouse, but it's not in our DNA. We don't wear trendy clothes, or sneakers paired with suit jackets," one of its executives explained to me. If the company is going to achieve its vision, he added, it needs to change its mindset and culture. "We have to change the way we think, the way we talk to customers, the way we talk to each other, and even the way we dress."

If you have tried and failed in the past to make the leap to an important new capability, that doesn't mean it's not going to work for you *now*. Just because you couldn't do it in the past, doesn't mean that you can't do it now, or that you can't do it in the future. *Figure out what you need to learn to be successful, and set out to learn it.*

Set big goals for what you need to learn, and then put the pieces in place to get to where you want to go. There are a variety of different ways to learn, including:

- **Share and cross-pollinate.** Conduct classes, workshops, webinars, mentoring, best-practice sharing, and training programs. These bring in ideas from outside, and spread ideas, skills, and knowledge within your company.

- **Develop prototypes (and not just of products).** Gain feedback by developing prototypes or proofs of concept, and getting them into customers' hands fast. These need not be fully functioning or formalized to be effective. In fact, simple, crude prototypes are often *more* effective, because people are more comfortable criticizing or even outright rejecting them. (Believe me, you'd rather a customer reject an early stage prototype than a more fully developed product that you've invested substantial time and money in.) Prototypes can be used to test product enhancements, new services, and even the language you use when interacting with customers.

- **Experiment with new operational approaches and ways of getting work done.** Healthy companies question the status quo and experiment constantly, even with mundane aspects of their operations. How often have you been asked to attend a regularly scheduled meeting (for example, every Friday at 9 a.m.) that probably made sense at some point in time, but now serves no purpose, or could be covered in just 10 minutes, rather than the allocated hour? (I call these "vestigial" meetings. Like an appendix, they no longer serve any useful function.)

- **Use mergers, acquisitions, and corporate venturing to gain new capabilities.** Corporate venturing is a powerful tool for innovation, and, if managed well, acquisitions can be a marvelous way to acquire new capabilities and new people that will enliven and enrich the dialogue in your company.

- **Recruit new employees who have the capabilities and knowledge to move your organization forward.** Hire employees who have the capabilities and values that you would like the entire organization to shift toward, who will be passionately committed to making your vision a reality, and who will accept a few setbacks along the way. I spoke recently with an executive who was recruited into her organization to implement a bold, new strategy. As a "new thinker," she repeatedly clashed with the old-thinkers in the organization. She persevered, compromised here and there, and acted on every opportunity that came her way to help employees gain new skills and mindsets. In time, she became highly successful and helped the organization to grow important new capabilities.

- **Partner.** Choose investors, suppliers, technology partners, and channel partners that fill capability gaps or that can help you build internal capabilities. One client commented, "We find partners who are highly capable in skills we don't have, and learn from them over time. They keep growing as we grow."

- **Pick your customers wisely.** Attract customers from whom you can learn, and engage them in the process. Workday, a provider of human capital management systems, opened its design partner program to a select group of customers, hoping to find customers that would be willing to share candid feedback on their use of learning applications. The eight selected design partners, including Four Seasons, CareerBuilder, and others, have actively engaged in Workday's program, leading to numerous lessons learned.

If You Want to Be Fast, Learn Fast

Focus your agility where it counts, and set specific learning goals. Learn deeply in a few areas rather than trying to learn in every single area of your business. Spreading your resources too thin over too many areas is counterproductive.

Fast-learning companies and people are clear and focused about what they want to learn. For example, one company that I worked with would like to develop predictive analytics as a competitive advantage. They will be successful if they are clear about what they would like to predict, using what data, and for whom.

Unfocused learning is inefficient, and takes away from getting the basics right for your customer. Remember: You still need those parts of your business that do the basics right and efficiently, day in and day out, to remain effective, such as delivering packages on time to the right addresses, ensuring that flights arrive safely and on schedule, keeping the store shelves stocked, processing customers' orders correctly, and so on. So, you need to figure out *what* you need to learn and focus your learning in specific areas. Figure 7.2 depicts a three-step process you can use to set learning objectives.

If you want to learn fast, there are three steps that will help get you on your way quickly and effectively.

Step 1. Anticipate the changes that may occur in your business environment. First, examine the trends you see and recent events that have occurred. Then, based on what you see in the environment around you, anticipate what *might* happen next. Describing three or four potential future scenarios is a powerful tool for opening up your thinking about the range of outcomes that may occur.

Here are a few questions to get you started:

- How might your customers' needs, values, and behaviors be different in the future?
- How will technology change what you and your competitors can offer?
- What new business models and new competitors could enter the picture?

Figure 7.2:

Setili Process for Setting Learning Objectives

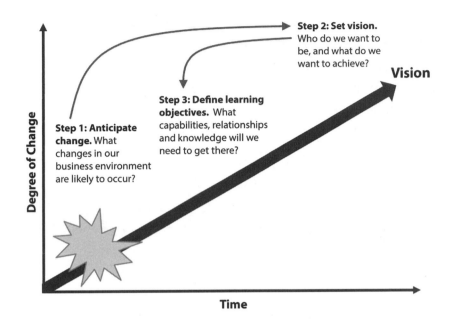

- What new regulations might be coming? Might some existing regulations be changed, or even eliminated? What will this do to the competitive environment, and how will it affect customer needs?

For more information, see Chapter 5 of my book *The Agility Advantage*, which provides techniques for anticipating changes in your business environment, and Chapter 7, which gives an example of how to effectively use scenario analysis. Visit *www.setili.com/frame works* to download valuable frameworks for anticipating change.

Step 2. Describe your vision, or desired future state, in vivid terms. Given the changes you anticipate in your business environment, paint a picture of what you would like your business to look like in the future, and what you hope to achieve. Illustrate the value customers will get from your offering, and how you will interact with customers and partners. Describe the distinctive capabilities, relationships, and reputation that your organization will have.

Step 3. Set specific learning objectives. Describe the capabilities, relationships, and knowledge you will need to reach your vision, given the business environment you will likely be operating in.

The following questions may be helpful thought-starters:

- What new product and service offerings will you need to develop, given the changes you anticipate in customers' needs, values, and behaviors?
- What new skills must your sales force acquire?
- What do you need to learn to build the type of customer relationships you envision?
- What technologies should you be experimenting with now?
- What alternative business models should you begin to develop and test?
- What do you need to do now to be prepared for the new regulatory environment that you expect?

The Remarkable Power of Setting Learning Goals

An industrial products company I work with was frustrated because each of their 5,000 customers bought only one or two products out of a selection of hundreds of SKUs. The company wanted to shift to selling a bundled set of products. The idea was that if customers would subscribe to a complete solution—a portfolio of proven products and services that worked well together—then customer productivity would be measurably better. With this reduced downtime and improved productivity, customers could focus on serving *their* customers, while my client made sure their operations ran flawlessly.

The trouble was that my client had few customers currently operating in this way. They knew that they had many things to learn to achieve their vision, so my client set specific learning goals. Here's a sampling of what they set out to learn, and how they accomplished this learning:

- Which products work best together to bring about the desired productivity improvement?
- Which types of customers are most amenable to a bundled solution?
- What is the best way to "prove" the productivity-enhancing value of a bundled solution? What results or test would be believable to prospects?
- How would the role of the sales representatives and service technicians need to change to make the bundled solution successful?

Once the management team laid out these specific learning goals, they were then able to develop a strategy for achieving them. They selected 12 customers, four from each of three different customer segments, and approached them with an idea: "Would you like to achieve a productivity improvement? Would you be willing to work with us to test different product combinations, and to quantify the benefit of a bundled approach?"

Only three of the customers bought into the idea, but throughout the course of a six-month period, a series of trials were run. My client learned in the first few trials at customer sites that customers measure productivity not in terms of output per hour, but in cost per unit. With this knowledge in hand, they learned how to conduct the trials to provide irrefutable evidence of the favorable impact on cost. Two of the customers achieved remarkable results and were willing to share these results in a case study that my client could publicize—a big win.

By being very specific about what they wished to learn, the management team was able to embark on a series of steps to reach their goals. As you set your own learning goals, the following two actions will help you achieve *your* goals.

1. **Adopt an action mindset and take action immediately to begin learning.** You can learn faster if you start learning immediately, and not waste too much time making *plans* to learn. There's no market research that can tell you what a customer is actually going to be willing to pay for. You have to get out there and find out for yourself to learn what customers are going to do.

2. **Be persistent.** When I first tried kiteboarding, I wasn't a particularly fast learner. My enthusiasm and persistence, however, were off the charts. Wild crashes and being dragged through the water gasping for air only made me more determined. I've tried something new every time I get out on the water, and as a result, I have achieved things I never thought I would be able to do. Companies that are persistent in pursuing their learning goals, that dust themselves off after failures and get right back to work, gain new capabilities fast.

Design Your Processes to Maximize Learning

A company I once worked with set a goal of growing sales by repurposing existing products and selling them into a market with which they had no experience or knowledge. Their inclination was to sink a lot of time and money into developing slick, sophisticated marketing materials and fancy presentations that described the value proposition in detail.

"Instead of all this marketing material," I suggested, "go visit customers with a whiteboard marker in hand. Enlist customers in co-creating the new product with you. Learn what the customer is trying to accomplish, and what drives their economics. You'll learn more by engaging customers in your learning journey than by trying to guess what the customers need."

When employees have an easy, intuitive way to share their knowledge with one another, to collaborate and advance your company's knowledge, they will. PayPal created a private Facebook group where employees can connect to solve work-related problems, and where they can learn from invited experts. The company also uses Twitter's Periscope live video service to enable employees to view and create short videos to increase their skills (after all, the best way to learn something is to teach it). By taking advantage of social media platforms that employees were already accustomed to and in the habit of using, they encouraged employees to work together and to learn.

Restructure for Learning

Choose the right organizational structure to meet your strategic and learning goals. For example, one company I know gained speed and agility by forming a partially autonomous "startup" within the larger organization. Freed from the normal corporate structure, the startup gained capability fast. Another company built capability by centralizing a formerly decentralized function to put greater focus on skill-building in that area.

When I was a young engineer at Kimberly-Clark, I was part of a task force of employees selected from plants all across the company. Our assignment was to increase production rates by 15 percent with little to no capital investment. It was a temporary, cross-business unit organizational structure created to address a specific opportunity.

By learning together, we built new capability, and created a lasting network of collaborators.

Align Performance Metrics and Incentives With Learning Goals

Incentives set up to motivate business units to achieve specific financial numbers often have the unexpected result of disincentivizing learning. If you say, "You must grow 5 percent this year to earn your bonus," you may find that employees meet the goal, but fail to learn and prepare for the future. For example, business units that are determined to hit, say, a 10 percent revenue growth goal, do so through brute force. They cut price or hire more sales reps, but they learn little about what customers want "10 percent more of."

In fact, desperation to meet financial targets can *destroy* knowledge. If we give every customer a low price, for example, we will never discover who values us the most. If you're in a fast-moving market and need to learn fast, design your incentives to encourage, rather than discourage learning. Set specific learning goals as part of your performance management and incentive system. We can be just as disciplined in setting specific learning goals, and measuring whether we met these goals, as we are in using financial metrics.

I once worked with a company that had the long-term goal of entering a new market. One of the most important determinants of success was designing the right product offering, and then setting up the operational capability to deliver that product cost effectively. As a first step, they created an early version of the product to show to customers and gain their feedback. The manager told his team, "We're not setting revenue objectives. I just want you to present this potential new product to 25 prospective customers." He added that the goal was not to bring in immediate sales, but merely to learn. A "win" would be to find out how interested customers were in the product, how they would use it, and how much value it could potentially create for them. "If you sell something, that's great, but what we really need is the knowledge and learning, to guide the next step of our product-development process." This was a brilliant approach. Rather than using a hard-sell approach, pushing a product on customers that might not be a good fit for their needs, the team focused entirely on learning *with* the customers. The end result was that the company gained the knowledge they needed, brought the right product to market, and enjoyed a very successful entry into the new market.

Send a Scouting Party

Explorers entering new territory send ahead a scouting party. This small group travels light. They find the pass through the mountains, the safest place to ford the river, where the dangers lie, and where food and water can be procured. They return with this information, and then the entire expedition can proceed more efficiently and safely.

Similarly, experiments and pilots are crucial for testing the waters when heading in a new strategic direction. By experimenting, testing, and making small bets, we learn the best path forward without risking the entire business.

When a company I know decided to enter a new market, they first assigned a small group of employees to create prototype designs and test them with customers. Their initial designs were all wrong, but they learned fast, with minimal risk to the core business.

Establish Feedback Loops

The most important element of learning through experimentation is establishing and monitoring feedback loops. Too often, I see companies trying a new way of doing something without collecting feedback to determine whether or not the change was successful. They launch a new product but neglect to ask the customer, "What happened? Did you like the product? How did it perform?" Or they implement change in operational procedures without documenting before-and-after results.

There's nothing worse than slogging away to head in a new direction or learn a new skill with no feedback regarding your progress. Design natural feedback loops into the work of your company so that employees can feel and see progress toward their goals. I stayed at a hotel recently that was trying to improve its scores on TripAdvisor. Whenever a new review was posted by a customer, the manager walked through it with the service staff so everyone would learn what customers loved about the hotel and what could be improved. A recent review read: "Very sincere and friendly staff. Especially Joyce, who is in charge of the breakfast area. She keeps the food items well stocked, and she is a most courteous, friendly, and helpful person. She always had a smile for everyone! Thank you Joyce!!!" Performance improves fast when there is frequent and specific feedback on progress.

When I worked as an engineer in a Kimberly-Clark production facility, I implemented statistical process control so that the employees running the machines gained feedback a few times each hour about quality, productivity, and waste. The feedback enabled the production team to learn quickly. If they saw a data point that was out of spec, they would ask themselves, "What changed?" Sometimes it turned out to be something subtle and undocumented. Once, someone had left the back door to the plant open, and the wind had impacted the process negatively. Another time, a rainstorm had just begun, raising the humidity in the plant and upsetting the process. Having continuous and immediate feedback enabled us to identify the causes of problems in a way that would have otherwise been impossible. It also prevented us from overreacting to normal fluctuations in the process, which could have sent us spinning out of control. Figure 7.3 illustrates the power of collaborative, fast-feedback learning.

When you experiment, you'll encounter failure, and you'll encounter results you didn't expect. That's a good thing, and a natural part of the experimentation process. You've got to be willing to accept the unknown as a part of learning, and have the courage and fortitude to keep moving forward regardless. As a ski instructor once wisely told me, "If you're not falling, you're not learning."

Figure 7.3:

Impact of Goal-Setting, Collaboration, and Fast-Feedback on the Learning Curve

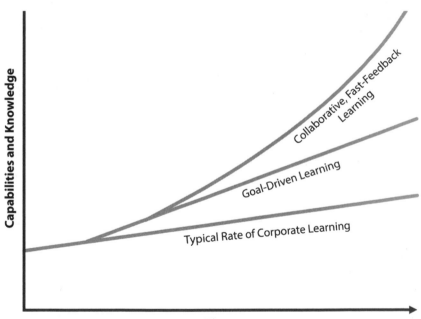

Have a Beginner's Mind

Getting the most out of learning requires awareness that you don't have all the answers, openness to being surprised, and a willingness to change your perspective on what you *think* you know. Awareness of your ignorance is your biggest advantage in learning.

Founders of the Casper mattress company decided to rethink the fundamental assumptions being made in the mattress and bedding industry. The pervasive wisdom was that consumers wanted a mattress designed for their specific sleep style. Hence, the industry was constantly bringing out products like the Sleep Number bed, and introducing myriad products with different padding, materials, and adjustable features. Casper's founders went back to basics, rapidly testing different materials and designs in an R&D lab that could mimic any possible sleep environment in terms of temperature, humidity, and other factors.

In addition to mattress designs, the team also tested sheets and pillows. Challenging the assumption that high-thread-count sheets equated to higher quality, Casper's tests proved that densely woven sheets impeded airflow, making sleepers feel hot and humid. Low thread count, it turns out, is both cheaper and more comfortable. Based on the sleep quality they observed, the company innovated "the perfect mattress, sheets, and pillow for everyone." Its back-to-basics design process, combined with partnerships with retailers like West Elm, and strong word of mouth and social media evangelism marketing, have fueled the company's rapid success.

Keep Your Acquisitions Vital, and Learn From Them

Acquisitions can be a wonderful way to acquire new capabilities, but too often, companies squander what they have purchased. The imposition of big-company policies and processes can dampen the entrepreneurial spirit and slow innovation. It's not uncommon to have the life squished out of an acquisition.

Microsoft's favoritism toward internally developed solutions has, in the past, caused the value of some of its acquisitions to be destroyed. "We did not get everything right about our culture," CEO Satya Nadella said in an interview with the *Wall Street Journal*, "especially around learning from others. Otherwise, why would we miss big trends?"[6] The article reported that "billions of dollars evaporated" following some of Microsoft's acquisitions. The company is improving, however, by integrating employees brought in through acquisitions into the leadership team, and employing them as change agents.

Employ Corporate Venturing to Bring New Ideas Into the Organization

The top executives of shipping giant UPS know that their business needs a constant infusion of new ideas from outside of the organization. With more than 434,000 employees around the world and more than $60 billion in annual revenue,[7] UPS is great at managing efficiency—down to the nanosecond—and it has deep internal expertise in logistics and distribution. To augment its internal knowledge and learn about emerging technologies and business models such as 3D printing, drones, and collaborative consumption, UPS invests in startups.

Rimas Kapeskas is managing director of the UPS Strategic Enterprise Fund, the private-equity strategic investment arm of UPS, which was founded in 1997. The Fund is a corporate venture capital group that focuses on developing partnerships and learning from investments in technology companies and emerging market spaces.

Prior to his role managing the Strategic Enterprise Fund, Kapeskas was in UPS's research and development group. Given his R&D background, focusing the Strategic Enterprise Fund on learning came naturally to him. "UPS looks for 'knowledge returns' as much as it does financial returns," says Kapeskas. "While we do make money on our investments, the more important goal is learning. By investing in startups, we enable UPS leaders to make better decisions, which is invaluable."

Continues Kapeskas, "Warren Buffett says to invest in what you know, but we try to invest in things we do *not* know. We need to have ways to learn about things in the marketplace that will affect us and our customer base."

Here is a sampling of UPS's Strategic Enterprise Fund investments:

- **CyPhy Works** is an innovative producer of unmanned aerial vehicles (UAVs), otherwise known as drones. Though the relationship is still in its infancy, the objective is to collaborate in the development of UAVs built specifically for assisting with package delivery. The use of UAVs for package delivery fits a number of service profiles. For example, an autonomous vehicle could be used in rural locations to reduce the cost and energy needed to reach the customer, or in hard-to-reach locations to deliver humanitarian supplies.

- **Kabbage's** innovative small-business lending model uses real-time data such as shipping volume and activity on eBay, Amazon, Square, and QuickBooks to make credit decisions. The synergy between UPS and Kabbage is strong: Kabbage's small-business customers share UPS shipment data as evidence of their ability to repay loans, whereas UPS uses Kabbage algorithms to decide how much credit to extend to its own small-business customers.

- **Fast Radius** uses 3D-printing technology, sometimes called additive manufacturing, to make everything from museum pieces to rocket parts. By co-locating at UPS's Louisville air hub, the company can make and deliver parts and products—overnight, if necessary. This arrangement benefits Fast Radius, UPS, and their customers.

- **Peloton Technology** is a connected and automated vehicle technology company focused on improving safety and efficiency in the trucking industry. UPS is the first carrier to test "platooning" capabilities for its extensive fleet of tractor-trailers, whereby braking, acceleration, and safely systems are linked between two or more trucks. Benefits include a reduction in collisions and related expenses, and fuel savings from improved aerodynamics.

UPS is actively engaged with the startups it invests in. At minimum, a UPS leader sits as an observer on the board of the startup, and sometimes UPS takes a full board seat. Perhaps more important, however, is that UPS collaborates with the startups. Says Kapeskas: "We look for interesting use cases that we can engage *with* the startups to leverage and apply what they are doing." Kapeskas introduces startup leaders to relevant groups and individuals within UPS so that these groups can partner with the startups on projects, embark on growth initiatives, or just interact informally. UPS people who are involved with the startups become a channel to the rest of the UPS organization, providing a window into how new technologies are evolving. "Interacting with startups gives us exposure to new types of thinking," says Kapeskas. "Entrepreneurs iterate quickly. We can learn from that. It helps us figure out how to introduce more flexibility into our culture and ways of working."

Startups appreciate the chance to gain access to UPS expertise and resources such as its client base, public relations presence, global network, and more. For example, Fast Radius's founder and chairman, Mitch Free, frequently visits UPS field locations, where he speaks to UPS salespeople and customers about how Fast Radius's 3D-printing capability can enhance customers' speed in producing and shipping high-value, low-volume parts, products, and prototypes.

Ultimately, says Kapeskas:

> It's not how much you invest—it's whether you invest at all. Even if a corporate venture fund only invests a modest amount of capital, it can still gain insight into new innovations, and can better understand the way startups think and operate.
>
> I see companies making the effort to learn from particular startups. But if they don't invest in those startups, they don't get the full learning value. If you don't invest, your interaction with the startup often ends up being a one-time event. You go back to the office and try to tell your colleagues what you've learned, but those learnings don't stick.
>
> Investing in the startups that you want to learn from ensures that you stay involved with them for the long haul, through the ups and downs. As a result, you learn far more than if you did not invest.[8]

Corporate venturing is a very capital-efficient model for learning about things outside of your corporate status quo. Without investing in equipment or engineers, you can take a peek at potentially disruptive technologies, and new ways of engaging customers.

And it is not just UPS that is using venture capital to learn. Corporate venture capital funds account for almost 17 percent of total venture capital dollars invested. In 2014, this amounted to $5.4 billion in investments, spread among 775 different deals.[9] GV—formerly known as Google Ventures, the venture capital investment arm of Alphabet, Inc.—has to date invested in more than 300 companies. Why? To, in the words of GV, "push the edge of what's possible" in the fields of life science, healthcare, artificial intelligence, robotics, transportation, cyber security, and agriculture.

And to learn.

Recognize Small Wins, and Enjoy the Learning Process

Spot and shine a light on individuals and teams that show even small signs of progress in heading the new direction or who acquire an important new capability. If, for example, you are looking to reduce an engineering team's speed in designing new products from 18 months to three months, stop by their work area to thank them when they achieve a minor improvement—for example, getting a product out in 14 months. If a customer service team is working to improve delivery performance, recognize what they've done when they have taken the first step by figuring out how customers measure delivery performance. Do this often, and you'll accelerate progress toward your goals.

Expect Rough Patches

Prepare for the inevitable friction that will occur as your organization strives to gain new capabilities. Communicate transparently about the transition and provide a path for employees to acquire the new skills to succeed.

As Thomas Friedman says in his book, *Thank You for Being Late: An Optimist's Guide to Thriving in the Age of Accelerations*, when your world is being disrupted, the wrong response is to try to keep things as they were. This is analogous to keeping your paddle in the water to try to slow down when whitewater kayaking. What you should do is paddle as fast, or faster, than the current to keep stability. And we must be willing to experiment constantly, fail, and then learn quickly from our mistakes.

Challenge Assumptions and Change the Rules

As I explained in Chapter 5, Facebook invested $2.4 billion in growing its user base and content before becoming profitable. Its investment was not valued on Facebook's balance sheet in the traditional sense, but it paid off. The huge number of users and user content turned out to be the fuel that created healthy, sustainable, long-term growth.

Facebook's success was also built on the fact that it was not afraid to change the rules. It grew revenues by selling *less*.

According to CEO Mark Zuckerberg, his company's strategy of selling fewer ads was internally controversial, but it has paid off. *AdAge* reports that Google, Yahoo, and others are squeezing more ads into each page of their websites, while Facebook has decreased the number of ads its users see.[10]

For example, although Facebook showed 65 percent fewer ads in fourth quarter 2014 than the year prior, the average cost of those ads to advertisers was 335 percent higher. By decreasing the number of ads it sold, the company vastly improved revenue per ad while increasing the value it provides to both advertisers and users by reducing clutter and distraction. The net result: 53 percent higher ad revenue.

As a Facebook user, I'm happy because I see fewer, but more relevant ads. The advertisers are happy and willing to pay more because they know that their ads are reaching the right people at the right time, and getting more attention. Facebook changed the rules, adopting a strategy that was controversial internally, and challenged conventional assumptions.

In Conclusion

When you learn fast and fearlessly, you will bring new value to your customers more frequently, adapt more fluidly to changes in your business environment, and improve the ability to weather whatever disruption comes your way.

- **Achieve dynamic stability by learning continuously.** Constant learning increases your organization's resilience in the face of market change. Experiment, learn from successes and failures, and then apply your new knowledge to the next round of innovation.
- **Beware plateaus.** When you achieve a major learning goal, you may wish to pause to enjoy the fruits of your labor. This is risky. Leap to the next S-curve the moment you have achieved each level of success, rather than allowing yourself to plateau.
- **Anticipate the changes in your business environment, and set specific learning goals.** Set specific learning goals, based on the changes you anticipate may occur in your business environment. Learn deeply in a few areas rather than trying to learn in every area of your business.
- **Adopt an action mindset—take action immediately to begin to learn.** Once you know what you need to learn to be successful, start learning immediately, and do not waste too much time making plans to learn.
- **Design your processes, metrics, and organizational structure to maximize learning.** Incorporate your company's learning goals into your performance management systems. Choose an organizational structure that supports your learning goals. For example, you may wish to form a partially autonomous "startup" within the larger organization.
- **Establish feedback loops.** Build continuous and immediate feedback into your learning process and the work of your company so that employees see what's working, and what's not.

- **Have a beginner's mind.** Not knowing is your biggest advantage in learning, so be willing to abandon your assumptions and to relearn everything you thought you knew.
- **Get the most out of your acquisitions.** Acquisitions are a great way to acquire new capabilities, but too often, companies impose policies and processes that inhibit their ability to learn from the companies they acquire. Learn intentionally with an open mind from the companies you acquire.
- **Employ corporate venturing to bring new ideas into the organization.** Invest in startups to learn about things outside your company's core areas of expertise, including new technologies, new business models, and new ways of engaging customers.
- **Expect rough patches and recognize small wins.** When setting out to gain new capabilities and learning, it can be slow going. Prepare for the friction that may occur as your organization works to gain new capabilities. Recognize individuals and teams that show even small signs of progress in gaining new capabilities and knowledge.

8

Rule #7: Build Trust Into All You Do

Since the company's inception in the 1890s, Fairbanks Morse Engine has been a leader in diesel engine technology. Its huge engines, which produce up to 20,000 horsepower, serve in critical applications such as train locomotives, naval warships, and as emergency backup generators for nuclear power plants.

As Fairbanks Morse looked for new opportunities for growth, it learned of a company called Achates Power, which had innovated a new technology that substantially improved the fuel efficiency and emissions of a unique engine architecture that Fairbanks Morse had produced since the 1930s. Fairbanks Morse saw Achates Power's innovation as a possible route to growth.

According to Fairbanks Morse president Marvin Riley:

Achates was focused on small engines for the automotive market, while our expertise was in very large engines. By combining our expertise in large opposed piston, two-stroke diesel engines with Achates' technology, we would be able to serve markets that needed a fuel-efficient, highly reliable engine that meets modern emissions standards. Partnering with Achates was an ideal way to speed up the development cycle, to create a new engine that would fuel our growth.[1]

Fairbanks Morse entered into a partnership with Achates, the purpose of which was to take the Achates design for a small engine and scale it up to make a large engine, 200 times bigger than a typical car engine. The engine would be ideal for hospitals, industrial facilities, schools, and municipalities that had no source of reliable power. These facilities can use $3 to $4 million dollars a year in fuel, so the 10-percent efficiency improvement the new design promised would provide substantial value.

To pursue this goal, a new development group, led by Jim Connell, vice president of research and development, was created. The new team was housed in a separate building on the company campus, where they would be protected from the distractions of the core business, and where they could meet spontaneously throughout the workday to share ideas. According to Connell, "What makes this group different is that we have incredible trust. This comes from our openness, honesty, transparency, and respect for one another. We're all accountable for all our collective work."[2]

The newly assembled team worked hard for 18 months to design, procure, and assemble parts before they were ready for their first test of the scaled-up engine design. The technology was complex. Each engine had more than 5,000 parts, and when fully developed, would cost customers more than $1.5 million.

When the day arrived to start up the engine for the first time, the team was anxious to see if the machine they had invested so much time, brainpower, and energy into would work. Unfortunately, the engine exhibited a serious problem after only a few hours of operation.

"It was devastating, and the team was in shock," said Connell. "We realized that some of the technology in the Achates engine was not scalable to larger engines, and that we were in uncharted territory. All of a sudden, the learning curve got really steep. This experience really tested the character of the team."

Since then, the team has continually improved the design through a series of redesigns and tests. In the process, Fairbanks Morse has shortened their innovation cycle significantly, from six to seven months per iteration to just a few weeks. Connell explains, "We've evolved quickly. The engineers huddle up together and come up with solutions. They know there will be setbacks, but that they have support from top management. They know they can do this without fear, making decisions on their own." The Fairbanks Morse team enjoyed a level of trust—both within the team and between the team and other parts of the organization—that is uncommon in many organizations. To accomplish its goals, the Fairbanks Morse team had to trust and rely not just on people internal to the company, but on a dozen partners, including Achates, universities, suppliers, and engine design specialists.

"We believe in giving teams the resources and knowledge they need, then trusting them to get the job done," said Steve Macadam, CEO of Fairbanks Morse's parent company, EnPro Industries. "The Fairbanks Morse team has done a terrific job. They've developed new technology that is an important source of growth—a game changer for the company, and maybe for the industry as a whole."[3]

It's true: Trust equals speed. We can't move fast if we haven't first built a firm foundation of trust with our employees, business partners, customers, and the communities in which we work. Trust allows us to adapt quickly to the changes we see in the world, without worrying about whether or not our key stakeholders are going to be fully engaged and supportive of our initiatives. When we establish the powerful gyroscope of shared values, purpose, and ways of working together, our people stay engaged and motivated, our partners supportive, our customers loyal, and our communities welcoming. People debate and disagree, then join forces to get the job done.

In this chapter, I explore the nature of trust in our business relationships, how to harness it to increase the speed of innovation and growth, how to overcome the obstacles to trust, and some simple but powerful ways to increase trust.

Trust Is Increasingly Important, but Sometimes Missing

Trust has always been an essential element in business. It's the foundation on which business is done. You trust that if you pay someone a certain amount of money, they will do what they promise when they say they will. This trust involves making a leap of faith, being confident that the promises made by the other party are real and honest.

The connected world we live and do business in today requires more trust than ever before. Why? Because the world has become more connected, across wider geographies, and more disparate groups. When we do business online, we are connecting with people we don't know and trusting them with everything from our cars to our homes, pets, and businesses. The trust that businesses need to develop with customers, partners, employees, and others has expanded exponentially, and as leading-edge technologies such as driverless cars and artificial intelligence change life in ways we couldn't have imagined just a few years ago, the need for trust continues to grow.

Trust is what enables business to work, and it has become even more important now that people are:

- Connecting online to share homes (Airbnb) and getting in cars with strangers (Uber and Lyft).
- Hiring freelancers through platforms such as Upwork.

- Connecting important sensors and controllers on industrial equipment (such as GE's jet engines and power plants, and AGCO and John Deere's heavy construction and agricultural equipment).
- Relying on other customers for technical support, suppliers halfway across the world for manufacturing, and remote physicians for healthcare.
- Developing autonomous cars and automating work formerly done by people.
- Partnering on innovation, distribution, sales, and myriad other tasks.

Unfortunately, although trust is increasingly important, it's not always present.

Paul Zak, a professor at Claremont Graduate University, believes that building a culture of trust can turn an organization into a high performer. He cites a PwC global CEO survey that found that 55 percent of CEOs believe a lack of trust in business is a direct threat to their organization's growth prospects.[4]

A recent Ernst & Young survey of full-time workers in the United States and seven other countries found that 46 percent of the workers surveyed reported that they placed "a great deal of trust" in their employers, whereas 15 percent reported having "very little" or "no trust at all." According to Karyn Twaronite of Ernst & Young, the top five reasons cited for those employees who had very little trust, or no trust at all, included:

- Employee compensation is not fair.
- Employer does not provide employees with equal opportunity for pay and promotion.
- A lack of strong senior leadership.
- Too much employee turnover, both voluntary and involuntary.

- Employer does not foster a collaborative work environment.[5]

What Is Trust?

So, what exactly is trust in business, and how does it affect us on a day-to-day basis?

Interaction Associates and the Human Capital Institute (HCI) paired up to conduct research on these topics and more. According to their report, there are several definitions relating to trust that are important to note:

Trust: The willingness to put oneself at risk based on another individual's actions. **Organizational trust:** The extent to which employees trust others within their organization, based on:

- Consistency, predictability, and quality of work and actions.
- Ability and evidence of past accomplishments.
- Shared sense of commitment and responsibility to achieving a common goal.

Level of trust: The extent to which:

- People have a shared sense of commitment and responsibility within an organization.
- Individuals feel safe communicating their ideas and opinions among colleagues, peers, and supervisors.[6]

The study found some interesting differences between the levels of trust in high-performing organizations (those companies that had growth in profit of more than 5 percent over the preceding year) and low-performing organizations (those companies that had growth in profit of less than 5 percent, or negative growth, over the preceding year). Although 56 percent of employees in high-performing organizations agreed with the statement "Employees have a high level of trust in management and the organization," only 26 percent of employees in low-performing organizations agreed.[7] Clearly there is a link between trust and financial performance.

Leaders must work to reinforce and build the trust that exists between them and their employees, customers, vendors, board members, stakeholders, and the communities in which they work. And when you destroy trust, you can bet that employees and others will become disengaged from their work and from their employer, efficiencies will decline, and the organizational pace will slow.

Trust Increases Innovation Speed, Organizational Efficiency, and Growth

Almost every leader in every business today is looking for ways to operate more efficiently, and to increase the speed of innovation and growth. As we saw in the partnership between Fairbanks Morse and Achates Power, one way for leaders to achieve these things is to increase the level of trust.

An organization without trust is inefficient. It experiences many stops and starts, as people check to see whether they have the approvals they need, and as they verify that other people have done what they said they were going to do. In an organization with low trust, employees fear being the one to bring the "bad news." As a result, problems fester and grow, rather than being promptly addressed. Leaders are not confident to delegate, and employees hesitate to collaborate, unsure if they can count on others to do their part. People don't ask for help when they need it. There is a vicious cycle of failure to meet commitments, blame, and wasted time.

Everything operates more smoothly and efficiently in an organization with high trust. When a problem crops up, individuals promptly bring the problem to light, informing others, so that everyone can pitch in to get things back on track. When employees know that they can count on each other, they are confident to move much faster. The organization moves like a flock of birds, *coordinating almost effortlessly.*

In his book *The Speed of Trust*, Stephen M.R. Covey presents a formula to turn the seemingly intangible quality of trust into something quite tangible and quantifiable. Says Covey, "Trust always affects two outcomes—speed and cost. When trust goes down, speed will also go down and costs will go up. When trust goes up, speed will also go up and costs will go down. It's that simple, that real, that predictable."[8]

Luke Johnson is a British venture capitalist and serial entrepreneur. Says Johnson, "For commercial life to function at all, there has to be a general assumption of trust—that partners, staff, suppliers, customers, and the authorities will do the right thing by each other. . . . Those who are suspicious of everyone have to limit their ambitions, because they assume deceit is endemic."[9]

Consider a situation in which you have a minimum viable product and you want to give it to a customer to get their feedback so you can make improvements to better serve your customer's needs. If your people are afraid to hand the item over to the customer, fearing that the customer expects a perfectly buttoned-up product, or fearing that the customer may leak proprietary information about the product to competitors, your innovation process will be thwarted. This fear and lack of trust will slow down your company's innovation process and hamper your growth potential.

On the other hand, if your people trust the customer to keep the item confidential while providing you with vital feedback, then you can share more information with your customer, which would allow you *both* to be more innovative.

Trust is a two-way street. Not only do you have to have trust in others—customers, vendors, partners, your board, your employees—but you have to be trustworthy yourself. That is, you need to be the kind of person and organization others can trust. Just as you must do things that build trust with your people, so you must do things that build trust with people, businesses, and other entities outside your organization. To be trustworthy requires being honest, sharing your real thinking, and keeping your word.

How Fear Gets in the Way

Fear causes lack of employee engagement and communication up and down the chain of command, and slows down almost any form of execution as employees wait for executive decisions or approvals before taking action. Fear also causes us to be overly attached to old business models, stunting our ability to innovate and grow. Company leaders become afraid to take the risk of moving to something new. Because they are afraid to move, they fail to paint a compelling picture of the future. When there's no roadmap for where to go, many employees are happy to just pitch a tent and camp instead of pushing forward into new territory.

Just like riding a bike, once you get going, your forward movement gives you stability and resilience.

Fear makes us overly averse to risk, but if you have colleagues you trust, then you can be confident that your colleagues will do their part. When you have trust, you are more confident to try new things as a company, and to explore potential new paths to growth. You work more intimately with customers. You delegate more to employees, and give them more freedom. You let things organically transpire, knowing that you cannot plan everything in advance. When you're really hitting on all the cylinders with this new way of working, using the new rules of doing business, you can achieve dynamic stability. You will feel, and be, more protected from market upsets than before.

Psychological Safety

Debate and disagreement are important for making the right decisions and we must create an environment of psychological safety for this to happen. According to Amy Edmondson, a professor at Harvard Business School, psychological safety is a shared belief that the team is safe for interpersonal risk-taking.[10] When you have psychological safety at work, people feel comfortable to disagree and innovate. They get more done, have more fun, and make better decisions. This disagreement is vital to make the best decisions when faced with an uncertain future, where the best path forward is seldom obvious.

In my experience, there are three kinds of leaders.

1. **Roadblock leaders.** These are the leaders who fail to establish clear goals. They focus on compliance and grant limited decision rights. They feel that they must provide all the answers, and they ask few questions. Psychological safety in this leader's team is low.

2. **Distracted leaders.** These leaders may provide the initial go-ahead, but they fail to follow up with the required resources and support. They are haphazard in recognizing employees' progress toward goals, and they may even inadvertently punish failure, not realizing the chilling impact this has on employee courage and morale. They have a habit of getting distracted by the next new thing, so they allow initiatives to fizzle out. Although these leaders may view themselves as completely trustworthy, employees do not trust them to provide support through ups and downs.

3. **Effective leaders.** These leaders consistently set a clear and inspiring intent. They seek advice, ideas, and opinions from employees, and they aren't afraid to admit

that they don't have the answer to every question. They provide resources and support for good ideas, and they empower employees to make decisions and act. They provide employees with ample opportunities to gain new skills and try new things, and they recognize even small wins—offering their employees frequent and candid feedback on performance. Psychological safety and trust in this leader's team is high.

Good leaders create a safe place for their people to work. Trust in this kind of organization comes from the top. The leaders model behaviors that create a trusting environment, and reinforce others in the organization who do the same. In her TEDx talk, Amy Edmondson explained that there are three ways for leaders to create an organization that is psychologically safe for employees:

1. **Frame the work as a learning problem, not an execution problem.** "We can't know what will happen—we've got to have everyone's brains and voices in the game. That creates the rationale for speaking up."
2. **Acknowledge your own fallibility.** "You know you're fallible. Say simple things like, 'I may miss something, I need to hear from you. . . .' That creates more safety for speaking up."
3. **Model curiosity.** "Ask a lot of questions. That actually creates a necessity for voice."[11]

Creating a psychologically safe place for your employees to challenge one another, to freely create and innovate, to make mistakes, and to learn is critically important for any organization that wants to grow fearlessly. You get what you reward, so take a careful look at the behavior you are rewarding in your organization, and make sure it's behavior that creates psychological safety, not destroys it.

How to Increase Trust

Because trust is so crucial, it's fortunate that there are a number of relatively simple steps you can take to build trust in your organization. In a *Harvard Business Review* article, Paul Zak found through his years of research and surveys on the topic of trust that there are eight specific and measurable behaviors that leaders can engage in to foster trust in their organizations:

1. Recognize excellence.
2. Induce "challenge stress" by assigning a difficult but achievable job to a team or individual.
3. Give people discretion in how they do their work.
4. Enable job crafting by allowing employees to choose the projects they work on.
5. Share information broadly.
6. Intentionally build relationships.
7. Facilitate whole-person growth.
8. Show vulnerability.

Says Zak, "Ultimately, you cultivate trust by setting a clear direction, giving people what they need to see it through, and getting out of their way."[12]

Fairbanks Morse, the company I introduced earlier in this chapter, has built a team of people who trust one another. Because their trust is so strong, they can innovate fast and fearlessly. The company has been manufacturing engines for more than 120 years, and yet it has not lost its youthful spirit. It is now inventing new ways to work, new products, and new avenues for growth.

The Fairbanks Morse team exemplifies several principles for how to build trust.

- **The team is non-hierarchical.** Every team member feels free to ask the others for help addressing challenges, opportunities, and other topics any time during the day. The team sits together with the boss, VP of R&D Jim Connell, whose desk and cubicle is no larger or grander than the newly hired engineer fresh out of school.

- **The team shares information transparently.** They have quick, spontaneous meetings to solve problems. Everybody understands everybody else's piece of the design, so that they all can help each other when necessary. "We are all very committed learners," said Connell. "No one is married to their own idea. Our team meetings are about people teaching and people learning, so the collective IQ of the group continues to go up."

- **Music is playing all the time, and there is lots of laughing.** People love what they are doing, so employee turnover is zero. "Everyone feels accountable to their teammates—it's a case of 'everyone pitches, everyone catches.' Team members are driven, they have a high sense of urgency, but they're having fun. It's really about allowing people to seek their highest potential," says Connell.

- **Team members value the sense of community they have built.** When it's time to add a new team member, every single person on the team interviews them, and if any member of the team has a concern about the job candidate, the person does not get hired.

- **The team engages in non-work activities that build connections among team members.** These activities include not just dinners and ball games, but intellectual pursuits. Several times each year, the group reads a novel or narrative nonfiction book together, inviting a local literature professor to lead a weekly discussion group. "This is a time to spend time with people whom you deeply respect and care about, that has nothing to do with work," said Connell. "We learn how each other think, because we all read the same thing, yet have completely different observations about it."[13]

The trust the Fairbanks Morse engine development team built—among team members, with upper management, and with outside partners—enabled them to learn faster, and ultimately, will allow the company to grow faster.

I once worked with a senior leadership team at a different organization in which the members of the leadership team were not working well together. People complained of finger-pointing, and many felt that accountability was lacking. Each function blamed the organization's stagnant sales growth on the other functions. The level of trust was low. I was asked to help them develop a strategic action plan to increase accountability, teamwork, and trust. As I sometimes do, I used two exercises for building trust and accountability that I credit to Patrick Lencioni and his book *Overcoming the Five Dysfunctions of a Team.*[14]

The first exercise is as follows: Seat the team in a circle. Then ask the person in turn to say where they grew up, how many siblings they have, where they fell in the birth order, and the most difficult or important challenge they faced as a child. It doesn't have to be a deep or troubling challenge. It could be something as simple as "I struggled in school" or "I had an older brother who used to beat me up."

The second exercise takes slightly more time, perhaps one to two hours. Ask the participants to contemplate silently, and then write down the answers to the following two questions about each member of the team: First, "What is that person's single most important behavioral quality that contributes to the strength of the team?" And then, "What is that person's most important behavioral quality that detracts from the strength of the team?" A typical response to the first question might be "Susan always makes it clear what I should expect from her, which helps me plan more effectively," or "Bill has an incredible level of creativity, which creates enthusiasm in others." A typical response to the second question might be "Frank often doesn't contribute in team discussions, yet he sometimes voices concerns about others' ideas later on, one on one. I wish he would raise these issues when the group is together," or "Karen often fails to show up for our team meetings on time. This causes us to be unproductive, because she misses some key communications that we have to fill her in on later."

When I worked through this exercise with the senior team, the results were fascinating. Participants revealed things about themselves that no one else knew. One person said, "I had six siblings. Our house was noisy and crowded, and one sister or another was always borrowing my clothes." Then one of the other participants said in response, "So, *that's* why you hustle so much. I get it now." One person on the team had moved to a foreign country during high school when his parents had an overseas posting. He had had to learn the language quickly to fit in. This elicited the response "Now I understand why you're so good at communicating and getting people's thoughts out on the table."

Each person had their own unique story that explained why they were the way they were. And when we went around the circle, asking each person in turn to tell what behavioral qualities each exhibited that contributed to the strength of the team, it was a powerful exercise for everyone involved. We don't often tell others, especially the people we work with, what it is that we appreciate about them. We might thank them for taking care of something, or for doing a good job on a project, but we don't often go deeper than that. The result that day was that there were a lot of really nice, positive things said about these people who had been feuding with one another for months.

One person said, "You know, what I really appreciate about you is that when you say you're going to do something, it's definitely going to get done." Someone else volunteered, "What I really appreciate about you is that you will never turn down the opportunity to contribute. You always volunteer to help."

Once we primed the pump with each person telling the others the positive things, then it was time for each participant to tell the others what behavioral qualities detracted from the strength of the team. One participant told another, "You put so many things on your to-do list that some things never make it to the top of the list. You're so eager to contribute that you tend to overcommit." Someone else said to another participant, "When I come to you with a request, it can sometimes be hard to get a commitment from you. I suspect that's because once you say you're going to do it, it's definitely going to get done."

We did this exercise in the morning, and the rest of the day people were much more interactive and they contributed, volunteered, and collaborated more with one another. Afterward, the typical feedback I received from members of the team was "Wow. That simple little sharing exercise to increase trust was the best part of the session."

Creative Conflict Is Valuable and Can Enhance Trust

A sign of a company that has a lot of trust is one that has a lot of healthy debate and disagreement. In a *Harvard Business Review* article, authors Michael Tushman, Wendy Smith, and Andy Binns write, "Firms thrive when senior teams embrace the tension between the old and new and foster a state of constant creative conflict at the top."[15]

Amazon currently has 14 leadership principles, which, according to the company, Amazonians use "every day, whether they're discussing ideas for new projects, deciding on the best solution for a customer's problem, or interviewing candidates." The 13th principle on the list is "Have Backbone; Disagree and Commit."

Leaders are obligated to respectfully challenge decisions when they disagree, even when doing so is uncomfortable or exhausting. Leaders have conviction and are tenacious. They do not compromise for the sake of social cohesion. Once a decision is determined, they commit wholly.[16]

So, how do we enable a state of creative conflict, in which people have a backbone and are free to disagree? By building trust in the organization. This means developing policies that create and reinforce trust and allow it to grow. This means being transparent in all you do. It means being accountable and doing what you say you are going to do. It means being willing to go with the flow in a fair way so that, as things play out a little differently than either of you expected, you deal with the new information in a fair way. This means having clear values and adhering to them.

As Georgia-Pacific's Billy Medof says:

Our management philosophy is an attempt to take the very best attributes of free markets and apply them to a private firm. The translation is not always easy. For example, how do you translate a basic free market principle like "freedom of speech" to a company? At GP, it's not just encouraged, it's insisted upon that we respectfully challenge each other, that we speak openly, that we sit in meetings and contribute our perspective. We don't use the pocket veto.[17]

Building Trust With Companies Outside Your Own

An important part of doing business today is reaching outside your organization to share and collaborate, allowing and encouraging the flow of information between the parties. Such collaboration helps keep your intellectual capital fresh and keeps your organization vibrant. Collaboration can also be worrying. You might also be entering into new arrangements that are unknown and ill-defined, because the world is moving too fast to nail the arrangements down with any degree of precision.

This, of course, requires no small amount of trust.

As we explored in a prior chapter, there are six areas in particular in which sharing and collaborating with others outside your organization can help you bring ideas to fruition. These include sharing of assets, technology, knowledge, data, talent, and relationships. Each of these requires a high level of trust to be successful.

For example, trust is crucial when you share your valuable assets, whether hard assets such as equipment, vehicles, and buildings, or soft assets, such as your data or brand name. Cinnabon has enjoyed healthy growth by allowing its valuable brand name to appear on Keurig and Pillsbury products, and even on popcorn. To be willing to put its brand at risk, Cinnabon needed to put the pieces in place to build trust with Pillsbury, Keurig, and other partners.

You will grow much faster and more fearlessly if you first establish trust when collaborating with entities outside your company, and when sharing things such as assets, technology, data, and knowledge. The elements of organizational trust outlined in the previous section were developed by Interaction Associates and HCI to describe the extent to which employees trust others *within* their organization, but they can also be applied to relationships *between* organizations.

Here are a few questions and issues to consider when collaborating with people outside your company, related to the elements of trust identified by Interaction Associates and HCI:

- **Consistency, predictability, and quality of work and actions.** When collaborating with others, what measures should you put in place to assure that your property is operated and maintained as you would yourself? If your brand is going to be used in conjunction with another company's product, as Cinnabon's is used on Pillsbury and Keurig products, what steps should you take to be confident that the co-branded product will be high quality, safe, and consistent? Once you have established this trust, both sides of the partnership can invest with confidence to grow fearlessly.

- **Ability and evidence of past accomplishments.** What reviews, references, and evidence should you rely on to be certain that your partner can and will do what they say they will, and that they are worthy of your trust? Should you run a trial or pilot with them, so both sides can become more confident in each other's ability to perform as intended?

  Once this confidence is established, both parties can act more boldly and efficiently.

- **A shared sense of commitment and responsibility to achieving a common goal.** It's well worth taking the time up-front to agree on concrete goals for the partnership, and to communicate these goals to all relevant individuals and groups within both partner organizations. Once goals are established, both parties should agree on the commitments, investments, and activities each side will contribute to pursue those goals. Having this trust-reinforcing structure in place becomes especially crucial when unanticipated events occur. When the unexpected happens, goals are clear to both sides, and each can act to respond appropriately.

Collaboration and sharing with others outside your company can initially seem risky, but in the long run, they reduce your company's risk. By co-creating with customers, building relationships with universities and researchers, creating platforms for others to interact with you, and sharing knowledge and ideas with third parties, you will stay much more in touch with the market and will be much more prepared for the future.

In Conclusion

In business today, trust drives speed, efficiency, and growth. Trust exists when people have a shared sense of commitment and responsibility within an organization, and when they feel safe communicating their ideas and opinions. Without trust, organizations become dysfunctional, just like the people who lead them.

Trust starts at the top. Leaders must trust those they work with, and who work for them, and they must model this behavior and reward and encourage it throughout the organization. Building trust will benefit your business, your people, your customers, your vendors, and others. As you work to build trust in your organization, keep the following points in mind:

- **Understand how trust speeds innovation and growth, and improves efficiency.** One of the most effective ways to increase the speed of innovation and growth is to increase trust in an organization. Similarly, trust between organizations enhances the effectiveness of partnerships and collaborations. As Stephen M.R. Covey explained, "When trust goes up, speed will also go up and costs will go down."[18]
- **Neutralize fear in your organization.** Make your organization psychologically safe for employees to voice their ideas and opinions, make decisions and take action, gain new skills, and try new things.
- **Take concrete steps to build trust.** Consciously and consistently do things that build trust in your organization instead of destroying it. Recognize excellence, give people challenging but realistic goals, grant people

discretion about how they do their work, share information transparently and broadly, intentionally build relationships, facilitate whole-person growth, and show vulnerability.

- **Encourage and expect creative conflict.** Debate and dissent are essential to fearless growth. Encourage employees to disagree and challenge each other.

Implementing Fearless Growth

In the previous chapters, I provided many examples of how organizations have used the new rules of fearless growth to improve their business results. This chapter is intended to guide you in the implementation process.

By implementing these rules, you will create an organization that is primed for fearless growth, in which everyone is aligned with your vision for the future and engaged in getting there.

As a leader, you have a number of decisions to make as you consider when and how to implement these new rules for fearless growth. Specifically, will you implement the new rules broadly throughout your entire company, or in just a few areas? When will you start implementing, and how can you best prepare your people, suppliers, customers, investors, and board for the changes your organization will be making?

One of Amazon's leadership principles, found on its website page "Our Leadership Principles," is "Bias for Action." Speed matters in business. The Amazon website explains this principle: "Many decisions and actions are reversible and do not need extensive study. We value calculated risk-taking." Amazon's perspective is that the occasional broken process or activity is worth the potential reward. I hope that you will adopt a similar bias for action, and will move boldly in implementing the new rules for fearless growth.

Two Things You Can Do to Get Started

I am often asked by leaders what two or three things they can do right away to begin the transformation process. Here are two things you can do *today* to get started:

1. Choose one or two parts of your business, and one or two rules

Rather than trying to implement the new rules across your whole business, which can be complex and overwhelming, start with one area. Choose an area with high growth potential, and in which your business environment is changing fast.

One client I work with chose to begin by implementing the new rules within just one of their many growth initiatives. The growth initiative they chose was a project focused on developing and deploying new mobile applications of their core product. Mobile is an area in which technologies and customer behaviors are rapidly changing, so company leaders knew that it was essential to make smart, fast decisions and to adapt quickly as the market changed.

For them, getting in sync with customers (Rule #2) was the most important thing to get right, so they focused there first. They implemented changes to get product ideas into customers' hands frequently, and established fast feedback loops so that product developers could rapidly introduce and refine new product features. This had positive implications well beyond the product development team. As a result of the fast feedback cycle with customers, the legal team could keep up with any contractual issues that arose, and the operations team could adjust their processes, responding to customer feedback. The company's customers appreciated the opportunity to be deeply involved in the innovation process because changes were required in their operations as well. And because the customers were able to see new iterations of the product frequently, they got started on making those operational changes immediately, rather than waiting until late in the process.

Pinpointing a few areas to focus on, as this company did, will lead to better results.

2. Write down changes you want to make to increase your business's success

When you picked up this book, one or two chapters probably caught your eye because they relate to a particular problem or opportunity in your business. Perhaps you feel that your business is too risk averse, and that if you were bolder, you could embrace and exploit the uncertainty in your markets (Rule #1). Perhaps you feel that you could move faster on your growth opportunities if you established partnerships to shore up a certain type of knowledge or capability (Rule #4). Or, maybe you see that you have not fully leveraged your ecosystem, and that there would be value in better connecting the people you do business with to each other (Rule #4). Wherever you feel your biggest opportunities lie, write down a few sentences about what you would like to change.

For example, one leader I know wrote, "Our growth initiative in the office furniture sector is stalled because there is a lack of trust between our company and the manufacturer who supplies the materials we use to fabricate the furniture. This problem causes us to routinely miss ship dates, so we're losing customers. I would like to build a more trusting relationship with the supplier to debottleneck growth in this sector."

Even if the problem or opportunity you wrote down is big and difficult to change, once you have written down what you would like to change, it's likely that the answers to *how* to solve the problem will become more obvious to you. You can then start working on the *how*, reviewing the ideas and examples in this book to develop a clearer idea of the steps you will need to take to achieve your goal.

Seven Steps to Determine the Scope of Your Implementation Process

The first step in implementing the new rules is to decide what your goals are, and what action you would like to take to reach those goals. The following questions can help you develop your plan.

Step 1: Identify areas in which uncertainty is holding you back (Rule #1).

As we discussed in Chapter 2, embracing uncertainty can bring you opportunity. Uncertainty and the fear that accompanies it have the potential to hold back your growth, perhaps significantly. Are there particular growth opportunities you would have pursued, had you been sure what to do, but you're just in a holding pattern, waiting to decide? Consider how you can address that uncertainty and risk, and then move ahead.

In 2010, after two years of shrinking profits, SAP leaders saw cloud-based software offerings such as Salesforce growing fast. SAP was the world's leading enterprise software and service company for "on-premises" solutions, and its business model was based on costly installations and license fees. Cloud offerings were becoming increasingly appealing to customers. SAP's leaders saw risks in the company's ability to continue to grow its on-premises software business. To address these risks, the company embarked on an aggressive series of acquisitions to become a leader in cloud-based software. Industry analysts questioned whether SAP could make the acquisitions pay off. A recent article in the *Financial Times* looked back at the period in which SAP made these acquisitions: The purchases unnerved analysts: Walter Pritchard, an analyst at Citi, said the "top dollar" acquisition of Concur came at a time when SAP's core business was not performing too well. Analysts were worried SAP was splashing out on something new in a desperate attempt to hide the problem.[1]

There were many doubters at the time, and SAP could have become paralyzed by uncertainty about whether its investments to grow the cloud business would pay off. Instead, SAP identified risks and uncertainties, and set out boldly to reposition itself as a cloud provider. This strategy has paid off. SAP's cloud business is driving robust growth and profitability for the company as a whole, and today, 76 percent of all worldwide business transactions touch an SAP system.

Step 2: Identify the most-important customers to get in sync with (Rule #2).

Who are your most forward-thinking and progressive customers, and how can you put a spotlight on them? Perhaps you could assign a special unit of your company to focus specifically on them, or maybe you could invite them to join an advisory board, or to partner with you on product development projects, or to undertake a new joint growth initiative.

One company I know identified eight major customers that it wished to focus its growth efforts on. These customers became intimately involved with the company's forays into new product areas and innovations.

Step 3: Identify areas in which you could benefit from partnering, borrowing, and sharing (Rule #3).

Is there another company that can help you move faster in your growth opportunities? Would partnering give you access to a valuable new distribution channel or manufacturing assets? Are there areas in which marrying your data with that of other companies could lead to breakthroughs? Is there a talent pool outside of your company that would be valuable to tap into?

LexisNexis, for example, aids law enforcement entities by linking together information on people, places, vehicles, and phones from more than 10,000 different sources. By bringing together disconnected data from many different sources, the company enables crime fighters to gain insights and linkages that otherwise might never have been seen.

Another company I know partners with universities to bring new knowledge into its development labs. A law firm and an accounting firm partnered to host joint events for current and prospective clients. Waffle House is partnering with package delivery startup Roadie. Partnership can take many different forms, and can grow your capabilities and growth prospects in many different ways.

Step 4: Set priorities for strengthening your ecosystem (Rule #4).

How might having a more vibrant ecosystem accelerate your growth? And how might you design, implement, and manage that ecosystem? Which person, people, or teams in your organization will be responsible for growing your ecosystem? Regardless of who is selected to lead the charge, every function, including marketing, legal, operations, and sales, will likely play a role.

OCEARCH, a nonprofit focused on improving the health of our oceans through research on apex predators such as great white sharks, has developed a robust ecosystem, with many different types of members.[2] OCEARCH expeditions generate open-source tracking data for shark research and for K–12 STEM education. The organization and its tagged sharks generated 6.5 billion earned media impressions in 2016, and have a legion of social media followers on Facebook, Instagram, YouTube, and top-10 ranked science app Global Shark Tracker.

The organization has created a powerful, symbiotic ecosystem.

- Brands including Yeti, Costa Sunglasses, Yamaha, and Caterpillar have contributed $40 million in funding for the expeditions and, in return, benefit from earned media.
- Researchers from more than 83 institutions have participated in OCEARCH expeditions, which serve as at-sea laboratories. Researchers collect data they could not have otherwise accessed, such as blood, sperm, and bacteria samples. More importantly, they make connections and collaborate in a way they never did before, sharing ideas and publishing joint papers.
- School children learn math and science using real-time tracking data from sharks that have their own names and Twitter handles. It is easy to imagine that the kids get more engaged in their math problems when they are talking about a real, 4,000-pound shark (like Mary Lee, Oscar, Grey Lady, or Cisco), and they can see up-to-the-minute information on where the shark is swimming.

- Professional fishermen manage the expeditions, and thereby contribute to saving the species they depend on to keep the ocean in balance.

Step 5: Identify what you can do to empower and inspire your employees (Rule #5).

In which areas of your business would it be most valuable to empower employees? How will you do so? Are there a few policies, processes, or messages you could change that would give employees the flexibility, power, decision rights, and resources to be more creative and effective?

In the same way that the Fairbanks Morse division of EnPro Industries gave its development team the space and freedom to invest in and innovate a new diesel engine design, are there teams in your company that would benefit from greater power and freedom to achieve growth and innovation?

And in the same way that SunTrust conducted a company-wide process to enlist employees in identifying and implementing game-changing improvements, could you do more to involve your employees in the business of fearless growth?

Step 6: Set learning priorities and debottleneck learning (Rule #6).

Next, consider what new capabilities your organization needs to have in the future. For example, you may think that new product lines and processes should be developed, or you may think that you need new professional services capabilities to grow. How are you going to get from where you are now to where you need to be in the future? What do your business, and your people, need to learn to get there? How will your organization gain the capabilities it needs?

Set specific learning objectives as a company. A business I'm familiar with set out to achieve specific learning goals in the health-care arena. By laying out these goals clearly, then creating learning-related performance metrics and accountabilities, and holding leaders responsible for achieving them, the company made significant progress each month in achieving its learning goals. In fact, occasionally, the company surged forward with a dramatic increase in learning.

Step 7: Take a few powerful steps to build trust within your company (Rule #7).

Is there anything you should be doing to build trust between the key players in your organization? It's hard to build trust across your entire organization all at once. But if you are focusing on a key area, there may be things you can do relatively quickly, such as providing opportunities for employees to interact in a different way, or helping them get to know each other's capabilities, strengths, and motivations better, or establishing norms for how you're going to work together.

A simple exercise such as the one I described in the "How to Increase Trust" section of Chapter 8 is a great place to start.

Communicate Your Vision to Employees

Implementing the new rules of fearless growth is exciting, but it can cause stress in the organization, and it may generate a lot of questions. For example, as you empower employees, more will be expected of them. As you work to get in sync with customers, you will have to get comfortable with the idea of releasing new products to customers in a less "fully baked" state than you previously did. As you make the borders of your company more porous, and get more deeply involved with outside partners, there will be questions about what to share, when. There could be legal issues related to intellectual property rights, liability, or other matters. Each one of these concerns, and the many more you are likely to encounter as you transform your organization, are real and require careful consideration.

So that employees in every function and business unit can work in a coordinated way to address these issues, it is important that you paint a vision of how you expect your company to change under the new rules, and what the business will look like in the future.

Jeff Immelt did a particularly effective job painting a picture of what the GE of the future would look like. For example, he found that he needed a new approach to attract more software engineers to the company, so he advertised for them on primetime TV. In a 2017 ad, GE asked the question "What if scientists were celebrities?" and featured Millie Dresselhaus, the first woman to win the National Medal of Science in Engineering. Immelt tried to change the image of the company, not just for customers, but for potential employees and partners. Immelt painted the vision for where he wanted GE to go before GE actually got there.

When you make changes to empower employees (for example, by granting them greater freedom to make decisions, or by putting new non-financial metrics in place), some employees may initially have a hard time adjusting. As Sir Richard Branson writes in his book *The Virgin Way*, "You can take the person out of the cage, but can you take the cage out of the person?"[3] He goes on to explain that when a person who is accustomed to a traditional corporate culture is given new freedoms, and absence of hierarchy, they sometimes have a hard time letting go of old habits.

I've observed this as well. When people are used to the boss making most of the decisions, they go to the boss for approval—even when the boss has explicitly told them they do not need to get approval. It can take repeated communication and reinforcement to change long-held beliefs and habits.

As you paint your vision, you can help employees get past their fears of the future by providing them with ways to better understand the uncertainties of your business environment, and to deal effectively with those uncertainties. Teach your people how to do simple scenario planning and sensitivity analysis so they can say, "The future's not completely predictable, but we can identify the things that are most likely to happen and we can plan for these." When your people gain experience thinking in this way, they become more confident, more prepared, and better at managing risk.

How Will We Know It Is Working?

People often ask me, "How will I know if the new rules are working?" Here is a list, by no means comprehensive, of the things you might watch for:

New Rule	How will we know it is working?
Rule #1: Embrace Uncertainty	• When you are confronted with a great deal of change in your business environment, have your people started asking, "How can we capitalize on this?" • Are leaders beginning to point out their own biases in making decisions, and are they working to overcome those biases? • When embarking on a new project, are teams identifying the assumptions and risks, and assigning explicit responsibility for managing these?

Rule #2: Get in Sync With Customers	• Have you had fewer product launches with disappointing sales results? • Have you been first to market with innovations more often? • Have B2B customers started asking you to collaborate? Have they shared their strategic direction, or even involved you in the process of developing their strategy? • Have consumers (B2C customers) started engaging more with you online (for example, posting product ideas, participating in forums, or sharing your news on social media)? • Have your leaders remarked more frequently about things they observed at a customer site? Have they recounted conversations they've had with customers? Do they seem to understand customer needs better than before?
Rule #3: Partner, Borrow, and Share	• Have some of your recent innovations originated with a technology or idea from outside your company? • Have you run at least one experiment in which you've combined your know-how, data, or knowledge with another company's to come up with a new insight? • Have you begun experimenting with using the assets of other companies or sharing your own assets (for example, office space, manufacturing capacity, brands, or intellectual property)? • Have you tried crowdsourcing or held a hackathon or contest?

Rule #4: Connect and Strengthen Your Ecosystem	• Have you organized any activities, online platforms, or other means to connect customers, suppliers, and other ecosystems with each other? • Have you noticed any examples of ecosystem members contributing things they would not have previously contributed (for example, helping another customer, providing you with a referral to a prospect, or partnering with another ecosystem member)? • Has anyone cited your strong ecosystem as influencing their decision to do business with you? • Are you beginning to experience a network effect, in which your ecosystem is becoming more valuable to its members as a result of having more members?
Rule #5: Open the Floodgates of Employee Creativity	• Have employees contributed ideas for improvement and implemented those ideas without being asked? • Have employees started pointing out things they are seeing in the marketplace, such as new competitor offerings or changes in customer preferences? • Have any teams spontaneously formed to solve a particular problem that your company is facing? • Are people from all functions in your company getting more involved in innovation? • Have you noticed more collaboration across business units and across functions?

Rule #6: Achieve Fast and Fearless Learning	• Do you have any new knowledge, capabilities, or intellectual property that did not exist before? • Have employees begun to be very clear about what the learning goals are for each project they undertake? • When a project or experiment is completed, are the results being widely shared? • Have you noticed excited conversations in the halls about new insights that an employee or team has discovered?
Rule #7: Build Trust Into All You Do	• Have you heard people saying, "I'll take responsibility for that" more often, and have you noticed that they accomplish what they promise more often? • Are you seeing more honesty, laughter, and requests for help and offers of help? • Have you noticed that fewer formal processes are needed for managing accountabilities, because work is coordinated, completed, and communicated in a more organic way? • Have you been hearing fewer complaints about work being late or incomplete, and more vocal appreciation among coworkers?

Adjusting Your Corporate Policies and Systems to Support the New Rules

Your company's metrics, capital funding processes, resource allocation processes, organizational structure, incentives, human resources strategies, and other policies and systems were set up to support the way you have done business in the past. You may find that the new rules call for new ways of working and different policies and systems. Implementing the rules may require you to rethink many of the things you are currently doing.

Choose the Right Metrics

If your business is like most, your performance metrics have been in place for decades, and they probably focus primarily on revenue and cost measures. To be effective in fast-changing business environments, you should also adopt metrics that measure and support risk-taking and experimentation.

For example, Ford Motor Company has historically measured executive performance based largely on the number of vehicles sold each year. Now, however, the consumer landscape is shifting and these metrics don't make as much sense as they once did. Fewer people are learning to drive and fewer people want to own a vehicle. Ford leaders know that the company must learn how to be successful as consumers shift toward shared vehicle ownership, autonomous driving, and the other innovations and industry disruptions yet to come. Vehicles may spend more time on the road, and less time in driveways. Vehicles must be built for durability, and for sharing. So, now, Ford measures its executives based on the miles traveled in Ford vehicles in addition to the traditional metrics. Because of these metrics, executives are incentivized not just to sell more cars, but to increase the lifespan and reliability of existing vehicles.

Make Budgeting and Project Funding Processes More Flexible

In traditional businesses, people were rewarded based on achieving revenue and profit targets set a year in advance. Annual reviews, performance appraisals, promotions, and pay raises all hinged upon a leader's delivery of predictable revenues and costs. The new rules require creating more flexible budgeting processes with money set aside for unexpected events. This enables fast approval of investment and resource requests when company leaders see a new opportunity they would like to pursue.

Provide Fast Feedback

In the new-rule scenario, you need fast feedback. This means having performance metrics that people can see quickly, even as often as every day. Speed is more important than precision. Interactive reports that allow employees to "drill down" into areas they are most interested in are ideal.

Consider New Business Models

Under the old rules, businesses made money by selling products and services. New business models are different, and there are new ways of making money. For example, sometimes you give something free to one set of ecosystem members, and earn money from another set of ecosystem members. Sometimes you offer a free version of your product in hopes that customers will upgrade to a paid version. There are many other models, but a common thread is that you have to be creative and ready to abandon some of your old ways of thinking.

Implement Metrics That Promote Cross-Functional, Cross-Business Unit Collaboration

Silo-specific goals and incentives can also be very effective in stimulating growth and efficiency by measuring each team's unique contributions. However, these silo-specific goals can cause individual business units and functional groups to make decisions that favor their own team, yet hurt overall company performance. For example, there may be a constant battle between the sales team, which tries to wedge rush orders into the manufacturing schedule so that they can meet their monthly sales quota, and the manufacturing team, which refuses to change the schedule to expedite even truly critical customer orders.

Therefore, when designing performance metrics, look for ways to motivate each team's unique contributions while at the same time driving overall company results. For example, a retailer might give its stores credit for e-commerce sales, and vice versa. Using geolocation technologies, a particular store might get credit for mobile and online purchases made by customers who had visited or were inside the store. Or the e-commerce group might get credit for a sale first researched online that was completed at the store.

Allow Ecosystems Time to Grow

Ecosystems can have a very long payback period. You invest up-front, and then wait for the seeds you've planted to germinate, grow, and bloom. The axioms that you've gotten used to in your core business (for example, "grow revenue at least 5 percent a year, and achieve at least 11 percent net income") may not apply here. Design your ecosystem so that as membership and participation grow, the ecosystem becomes more self-sustaining and generates money instead of costing money.

Implement Flexible Operations

Achieving fearless growth sometimes requires reconfiguring operations to allow greater flexibility.

One manufacturer I know was besieged by upstart competitors. The company needed to experiment more, learn faster, and get new products out into the market more quickly to defend its position in the market. The company was accustomed to running large manufacturing machines with massive economies of scale. Inserting a short run of new product into the production schedule was costly and was often nixed by the operating managers. After losing market share for months, the manufacturer installed a small, flexible line that could make small quantities of product without disturbing the big manufacturing machines that were churning out high-volume products at low cost.

Another company I know was in a service business. After years of losing money on small accounts, it instituted new streamlined procedures for serving small accounts. Doing so freed up service personnel time, so that they could lavish attention on their biggest customers. By creating several tiers of customers, each with different service expectations, the company became more efficient and more flexible to try new things. Growth became much easier to achieve, and the company flourished.

Allow for Flexibility in Partnerships

To spur fearless growth, you need to become proficient and fast at setting up simple agreements with your partners that leave flexibility for the unknown. You can't plan everything with your partners, and you can't predict everything that might happen. Sometimes it's better to get a simple arrangement in place with partners, and then adjust the arrangement as both parties gain experience. Agree on the objectives you're both working toward, and then figure it out together as you go.

Cultivate Flexible Supplier Partnerships

Create flexible supply chains that can turn on a dime. Treating your suppliers as partners means they can dedicate appropriate resources and become more responsive to your needs. In addition, you should be responsive to *them*. Establishing trust is key.

Why It's Worth It

The world is changing fast. Automation, digitization, and artificial intelligence are transforming our economy. At the same time, customer preferences, behaviors, and needs are changing fast. Regulations are struggling to keep up and are sometimes out of step with reality.

In the face of these changes, it's natural for company leaders to worry about whether they can maintain the growth and profitability levels that investors expect. It's natural for employees to worry whether they can keep up with the changes, whether their jobs will be eliminated, and whether new demands that are difficult to fulfill will be made. All these worries and fears are legitimate and rational.

I have developed the new rules laid out in this book so that company leaders and employees can employ new ways of working. It may be a bit daunting when you first implement the new rules. However, once you have implemented them, you will be safer and more resilient in the face of market upsets and disruptions, and you will have *less* reason to worry. Why?

- You will spot and capitalize on more opportunities, and you'll be more adept at managing risk.
- You will be in sync with customers, so you will never be blindsided by market change.
- Because talent, data, knowledge, and assets will flow across your company's borders, your intellectual capital and knowledge will stay fresh, vibrant, and relevant. You'll have partners that trust and support you.
- You may have an ecosystem of customers, suppliers, channel partners, content providers, and others that are strongly connected to each other, and to you. This ecosystem will be a self-sustaining driver of growth and learning.
- Your employees will be engaged and creative. They will be attuned to changes in the market and will act in the company's best interest, responding to market change in a fluid way.

- Your company's capabilities will continuously improve in targeted areas, and your people will be constantly learning and adapting.
- Your employees, leaders, partners, and customers will trust each other, so you can move fast and fearlessly.

Each of the new rules mitigates risk by helping you become more aware of and responsive to changes in your business environment. As a result, you will be able to build new sources of competitive advantage as you continue to grow.

Delta Air Lines provides a good example. Every large business touts that it is a great place to work, setting up recruiting sites with photos of happy employees doing fun things, and publishing their core values for everyone to see. However, there is often a big difference between how these companies present themselves and reality. This is definitely *not* the case with Delta Air Lines, the Atlanta-based airline with 80,000 employees serving more than 180 million passengers each year.

When Delta CEO Ed Bastian was asked by a reporter to describe his job in five words, Bastian's answer was simple: "taking care of our people."[4] This isn't just idle talk meant to give the airline's employees a short-term morale boost. Bastian and Delta Air Lines back up this simple strategy with concrete action. In 2017, the company paid out $1.1 billion in profit sharing to its people (an average of more than $13,000 per employee), and has given out nearly $5 billion over the past five years—more than any other corporate profit-sharing program, amounting to more than 20 percent of each employee's annual compensation in some years. The company also gives 1 percent of net income to charity. Delta makes a point of hiring "servant leaders," men and women who want to be part of the Delta family and are naturally inclined toward giving great service. Each of Delta's top leaders is assigned to an airport, which they travel to frequently to meet with Delta employees on the ground (and in the air) to get real-time insights into their challenges and opportunities.

Delta employees love the company and its unique, people-focused culture. On company review site Glassdoor, employees give the airline high marks. Out of more than 1,500 reviews, 95 percent approve of CEO Ed Bastian and 90 percent would recommend the company to a friend. The most-recent review as of this writing reflects the feeling of most: "Exciting work environment. Great, hard-working people. GREAT company."

Delta Air Lines is clearly doing something right. The company was named the number-one airline in Fortune's 2017 ranking of World's Most Admired Airlines, and was also included on Fortune's 100 Best Companies to Work For list, with 96 percent of employees saying "I'm proud to tell others I work here!" Taking care of employees doesn't cost money, it creates money. In 2016, Delta earned pre-tax income of $6.1 billion; far higher than its larger rivals American Airlines and United.

In Conclusion

I demonstrate in the pages of this book that adopting the new rules of business is essential for fearless growth. Some aspects of adopting the rules will be easy, and some aspects may be challenging. Once you start down this road, however, you will be more resilient than ever in the face of market upsets and disruptions.

You will be leading change instead of being whipsawed by it. Your employees will be aligned with your goals, fully engaged in their work, and acting in the company's best interest. You will create a rich, two-way street with your customers, and will be far less likely to be blindsided by changes in your markets. Your partners will support you, and you will support them, in a virtuous circle that will spark innovation. You will create an ecosystem that is self-sustaining and that drives your growth. You'll constantly learn and adapt as the business environment changes. And your employees, leaders, partners, customers, and communities will trust one another, which will allow you to move fast and fearlessly.

The new rules of fearless growth offer any company the opportunity to leap ahead of competitors. As you work to apply the new rules in your organization, be sure to keep the following points in mind:

- **The time to start is *now*.** There's every reason to start implementing the new rules now, and not to wait until "the time is right." Start small by choosing one or two parts of your business to focus on, or one or two rules to implement.

- **Set clear priorities for your implementation process.** Although the new rules for fearless growth are powerful, they can't do anything for you or your business if they aren't implemented. Implementation will be different for every business and for every industry. Decide in which areas of your business the new rules will have the greatest positive impact and focus your efforts there.

- **Communicate your vision.** Although business leaders should always communicate their visions for the future to their employees, customers, partners, and the communities in which they do business, this is especially true when you're about to embark on major changes to the way you do business. Get out front with your vision, and then follow with action.

- **Don't let your corporate policies and systems be a bottleneck to growth.** You can't implement the new rules without adjusting, and in some cases completely replacing your old policies and systems. This includes such things as choosing the right metrics, making

budgeting more flexible, providing fast feedback, considering new business models, and more.

- **Benefits of implementing the new rules.** Implementing
  the new rules for fearless growth can be daunting
  at first, but once you have made the changes, you
  will be safer and more resilient in the face of market
  disruptions.

CONCLUSION

When I sent the manuscript of my first book, *The Agility Advantage*, to my publisher, I already knew I would write a second book. I wasn't sure exactly what the topic would be, but I was certain that it would take the lessons I presented in my first book even further, responding to the needs of large businesses that are trying to learn lessons of speed and agility from the startup world.

As the idea for this book began to crystalize in my mind, I asked my clients, which include some of today's most successful large businesses, what obstacles they were facing and what they were doing to get over, under, and around them. The knowledge I gained from these hundreds of discussions with CEOs, company founders, executives, and more became the new rules of fearless growth, and the firm foundation on which I wrote this book.

My hope is that you will take these new rules to heart. But even more than taking these new rules to heart, I hope you will put them into action. Although some of the new rules might sound familiar to you, chances are you haven't seen them presented in quite this way, nor accompanied by these particular stories of leaders who are putting them to work in their organizations with tremendous success.

Although this last part of the book is called the Conclusion, I can assure you it is not The End. As a complementary supplement to this text, I offer a wealth of information—including frameworks, tools, techniques, and case studies—online for your use at my company website, *www.setili.com*. In addition, my consulting firm, Setili & Associates, is available to work with you if you have any questions about how to implement the techniques presented in this book. We have years of experience with some of the world's leading companies, including Delta Air Lines, Coca-Cola, Cox Enterprises, The Home Depot, Equifax, Fiserv, UPS, Walmart, and others.

To my great surprise, writing this second book was even more rewarding than writing my first. I hope you've enjoyed reading this book as much as I enjoyed writing it. I will have reached my goal if you put the techniques I describe in *Fearless Growth* to work in your organization, and as a result you find the success you are looking for. Please send me your success stories as your organization grows fearlessly and your people and customers enjoy the rewards; I can't wait to read them.

NOTES

Chapter 1

1. Alan Ohnsman, "GM May Soon Have 'Thousands' Of Self-Driving Electric Bolts In A Lyft Test Fleet," *The Little Black Book of Billionaire Secrets*, February 17, 2017.
2. Ibid.
3. Micheline Maynard, "Even Car Guys Say Their Teens Aren't Driving," *Forbes*, October 13, 2014, *www.forbes.com/sites/michelinemaynard /2014/10/13/even-car-guys-say-their-teens-arent-driving/#7b342bd227ad*.
4. Larry Copeland, "Many Teens Taking a Pass on Drivers License," *USA TODAY*, October 13, 2013, *www.usatoday.com/story/news/nation/2013 /10/13/teen-drivers-license/2891701/*.
5. Micheline Maynard, "Even Car Guys Say Their Teens Aren't Driving," *Forbes*, October 13, 2014, *www.forbes.com/sites/michelinemaynard /2014/10/13/even-car-guys-say-their-teens-arent-driving/#7b342bd227ad*.
6. Davey Alba, "The Lyft-GM Deal and Why You Probably Won't Buy a Self-Driving Car," *Wired*, January 2016, *www.wired.com/2016/01/the-lyft-gm -deal-and-why-you-probably-wont-buy-a-self-driving-car/*.
7. Holman W. Jenkins, Jr., "GM Says Au Revoir to Europe," *Wall Street Journal*, March 11–12, 2017.
8. Geoff Colvin, "Why every aspect of your business is about to change," *Fortune*, October 22, 2015, *http://fortune.com/2015/10/22/the-21st -century-corporation-new-business-models/*.
9. "The Creed of Speed," *Economist*, December 5, 2015.
10. Alan Murray, "Six fundamental truths about the 21st Century Corporation," *Fortune*, October 22, 2015, *http://fortune.com/2015/10/22/six-truths-21st -century-corporation/*.

Chapter 2

1. "Ratings agencies downgrade UK credit rating after Brexit vote," *BBC*, June 27, 2016, *www.bbc.com/news/business-36644934*.
2. John Dowdy and Kirk Rieckhoff, "Agility in U.S. National Security," in *America's National Security Architecture: Rebuilding the Foundation*, November 2016, *www.mckinsey.com/industries/public-sector/our-insights /agility-in-us-national-security*.
3. Jason Gay, "The World's Fastest Woman," *Wall Street Journal*, January 8, 2017.
4. Billy Medof, speaker at Setili & Associates Strategic Agility Think Tank event, May 24, 2016.
5. Brandi Quinn, interview, March 13, 2017.
6. Michael Lewis, *The Undoing Project* (New York: W.W. Norton & Company, 2017).
7. Ibid.
8. "Exploring Space Makes Life Better on Earth," *www.virgingalactic.com /why-we-go/*.
9. Michael Lewis, *The Undoing Project* (New York: W.W. Norton & Company, 2017).
10. John Antczak, "Space tourism companies employing designs including winged vehicles, vertical rockets with capsules and high-altitude balloons," *U.S. News & World Report*, February 15, 2016, *www.usnews.com/news /science/articles/2016-02-15/space-tourism-projects-at-a-glance*.
11. "Global box office revenue from 2016 to 2020 (in billion U.S. dollars)," *www.statista.com/statistics/259987/global-box-office-revenue/*.
12. Amanda Setili, *The Agility Advantage* (Hoboken, N.J.: Jossey-Bass, 2014), 159–160.
13. Patrick McGee, "SAP aims to pull Europe out of 'digital recession,'" *Financial Times*, January 25, 2017.
14. Adi Ignatius, "We Need People to Lean Into the Future, A Conversation with Walmart CEO Doug McMillon," *The Harvard Business Review*, March–April 2017, 84–100.

Chapter 3

1. Lindsay Chappell, "Nissan exec wants faster customer satisfaction feedback," *Automotive News*, August 6, 2014, *www.autonews.com/article/20140806/ RETAIL01/140809857/nissan-exec-wants-faster-customer-satisfaction -feedback*.
2. Andrew Hutchinson, "Big Brand Theory: Nissan Uses Social to Build Brand Authenticity," *SocialMediaToday*, May 18, 2015, *www.socialmediatoday. com/special-columns/2015-05-18/big-brand-theory-nissan-uses-social-build -brand-authenticity*.
3. Eddie Yoon, "Make Your Best Customers Even Better," *Harvard Business Review*, March 2014, *https://hbr.org/2014/03/make-your-best-customers -even-better*.
4. Patricia Rosenfeld, interview, November 8, 2016.
5. Elon Musk, Twitter, *https://twitter.com/elonmusk*.

6. "Fountain of Data: Coke Freestyle Dispenses Insights Along With Beverages," *Coca-Cola Journey*, October 31, 2014, *www.coca-colacompany.com/coca -cola-unbottled/fountain-of-data-coke-freestyle-dispenses-insights-along -with-beverages*
7. Thomas Friedman, *Thank You for Being Late: An Optimist's Guide to Thriving in the Age of Accelerations* (New York: Farrar, Straus and Giroux, 2016).
8. *Life* (October 9, 1939), 93.
9. Ibid.

Chapter 4

1. Leila Durmaz, "Lessons Learned from Successful Employee Suggestion Programs," *ESP Ninja*, May 9, 2014, *www.espninja.com/lessons-learned -successful-employee-suggestion-programs/*.
2. Eugene Kim, "Amazon just made thousands of books free for its Prime members—here's a simple reason why," *Business Insider*, Oct. 5, 2016, *www .businessinsider.com/amazon-prime-members-spend-a-lot-more-than-non -prime-members-2016-10*.
3. Adam Levy, "Instagram's Ad Revenue Could Surpass Twitter's This Year," *The Motley Fool*, July 24, 2016, *www.fool.com/investing/2016/07/24 /instagrams-ad-revenue-could-surpass-twitters-this.aspx*.
4. Thomas Friedman, *Thank You for Being Late: An Optimist's Guide to Thriving in the Age of Accelerations* (New York: Farrar, Straus and Giroux, 2016).
5. "Why giants thrive, The power of technology, globalisation and regulation," *The Economist*, Sept. 15, 2016, *www.economist.com/news/special-report /21707049-power-technology-globalisation-and-regulation-why-giants -thrive*.
6. Geoff Colvin, "Why every aspect of your business is about to change," *Fortune*, October 22, 2015, *http://fortune.com/2015/10/22/the-21st-century -corporation-new-business-models/*
7. Michael Tushman, "Leadership Tips for Today to Stay in the Game for Tomorrow," *IESE Insight*, 23 (2014): 23.
8. John Hagel III, John Seely Brown, and Lang Davison, "Abandon Stocks, Embrace Flows," *Harvard Business Review* (2009).
9. Geoff Colvin, "Why every aspect of your business is about to change," *Fortune*, October 22, 2015, *http://fortune.com/2015/10/22/the-21st-century -corporation-new-business-models/*.
10. Charles Duhigg and Keith Bradsher, "How the U.S. Lost Out on iPhone Work," *Pulitzer*, January 21, 2012, *www.pulitzer.org/winners/staff-74*.
11. Liz Gannes, "Tesla CEO and SpaceX Founder Elon Musk: The Full D11 Interview (Video)," *All Things Digital*, retrieved May 31, 2013.
12. Thomas Friedman, *Thank You for Being Late: An Optimist's Guide to Thriving in the Age of Accelerations* (New York: Farrar, Straus and Giroux, 2016).
13. Ibid., 69.
14. Nathan Furr, Kate O'Keeffe, and Jeffrey H. Dyer, "Managing Multiparty Innovation," *Harvard Business Review*, November 2016, *https://hbr. org/2016/11/managing-multiparty-innovation*.

15. David Lee, "Welcome to Innovation Friday," *SunTrust Bank*, August 22, 2015, *www.slideshare.net/heydavidly/welcometoinnovationfriday*
16. Ibid.
17. Ibid.
18. Ibid.
19. Ibid.
20. Hans Eckman, "Innovation Programs at SunTrust," Building Business Capability Conference, the Official Conference of the International Institute of Business Analysis, November 2–4, 2015, *www.buildingbusinesscapability.com/wordpress/wp-content/proceedings/2016/142.pdf.*
21. Mark Pearson, LinkedIn profile, *www.linkedin.com/in/markpearson/.*
22. *Banking Perspective*, Q1 2016, *www.theclearinghouse.org//media/tch/documents/research/banking%20perspectives/2016/q1/2016_q1_banking-perspective.pdf?la=en.*
23. *Ibid.*
24. Amar Toor, "Waffle House becomes an unlikely competitor to FedEx and UPS," *The Verge*, February 24, 2015, *www.theverge.com/2015/2/24/8098759/waffle-house-roadie-delivery-app-partnership.*
25. *www.roadie.com/.*
26. Graham Winfrey, "Peter Diamandis: Want to Be a Billionaire? Solve a Billion-Person Problem," *Inc.*, June 13, 2014, *www.inc.com/graham-winfrey/peter-diamandis-billion-dollar-problem.*

Chapter 5

1. Marc Benioff and Carlye Adler, *Behind the Cloud: The Untold Story of How salesforce.com Went from Idea to Billion-Dollar Company-and Revolutionized an Industry* (New York: Jossey-Bass, 2009), 48.
2. Ibid., 49–50.
3. "Join us at Dreamforce, the Largest Gathering of Media Industry Trailblazers," *DreamForce*, *www.salesforce.com/dreamforce/DF16/industries/media/#why.*
4. Laura Fagan, "The Salesforce Ecosystem Explained," September 1, 2015, *salesforce blog, www.salesforce.com/blog/2015/09/salesforce-ecosystem-explained.html.*
5. Klint Finley, "Salesforce Gives Every Company Its Very Own App Store," *Wired*, October 31, 2013, *www.wired.com/2013/10/appexchange/.*
6. Jason Bloomberg, "Salesforce Ecosystem: Growth Beyond The Cloud," *Forbes*, September 21, 2015, *www.forbes.com/sites/jasonbloomberg/2015/09/21/salesforce-ecosystem-growth-beyond-the-cloud/#4e223b536f60.*
7. John F. Gantz, Pam Miller, "The Salesforce Economy: Enabling 1.9 Million New Jobs and $389 Billion in New Revenue Over the Next Five Years," *IDC*, September 2016, *www.salesforce.com/assets/pdf/misc/IDC-salesforce-economy-study-2016.pdf.*
8. John Morrow, interview, February 23, 2017.
9. James Moore, *The Death of Competition: Leadership & Strategy in the Age of Business Ecosystems* (New York: HarperBusiness, 1996), 26.

10. Spencer E. Ante, "Amazon: Turning Consumer Opinions into Gold," *BloombergBusinessWeek*, October 15, 2009, *www.bloomberg.com/news /articles/2009-10-15/amazon-turning-consumer-opinions-into-gold.*

11. "Local Consumer Review Survey," *BrightLocal*, 2016, *www.brightlocal .com/learn/local-consumer-review-survey/.*

12. Jure Leskovec, "Web Data: Amazon Reviews," Standford University, March 2013, *https://snap.stanford.edu/data/web-Amazon.html.*

13. Tomas Kellner, "Everything You Always Wanted to Know About Predix, But Were Afraid to Ask," *GE Reports*, October 9, 2014, *www.gereports.com /post/99494485070/everything-you-always-wanted-to-know-about-predix/.*

14. Jeff Immelt, "Why GE is giving up employee ratings, abandoning annual reviews and rethinking the role of HQ," *linkedin.com/pulse*, August 4, 2016, *www.linkedin.com/pulse/why-ge-giving-up-employee-ratings-abandoning -annual-reviews-immelt?trk=prof-post.*

15. "Airbnb Experiences," Airbnb, *www.airbnb.com/experiences.*

16. David Zax, "Airbnb Now Offers 'Social Impact Experiences.' How Much Good Will They Do?" *Fast Company*, December 14, 2016, *www.fast company.com/3065925/airbnb-now-offers-social-impact-experiences -how-much-good-will-they-do.*

17. "Walmart & Sam's Club Consulting," *Enhanced Retail Solutions*, 2016, *www.enhancedretailsolutions.com/pdfs/Walmart_Consulting.pdf.*

18. "Innovation @Labs," *Walmart@Labs*, 2013, *www.walmartlabs.com /innovation/labs.*

19. "Team," *Walmart@Labs*, 2013, *www.walmartlabs.com/team.*

20. Billy Medof, speaker at Setili & Associates Strategic Agility Think Tank event, May 24, 2016.

21. "Apple's Worldwide Developers Conference Kicks Off June 13 in San Francisco," *Apple*, April 18, 2016, *www.apple.com/pr/library/2016/04 /18Apples-Worldwide-Developers-Conference-Kicks-Off-June-13-in-San -Francisco.html.*

22. "2016 WWDC Event Details Confirmed by Apple," Apple Toolbox, April 20, 2016, *http://appletoolbox.com/2016/04/2016-wwdc-event-details -confirmed-by-apple/.*

23. Brian Withers, "Fitbits Down, But With its Active User Community, it's Not Out," *Fox Business*, February 3, 2017, *www.foxbusiness.com /markets/2017/02/03/fitbits-down-but-with-its-active-user-community-its -not-out.html.*

24. Don Reisinger, "GoPro's next act: building an online entertainment empire," *Fortune*, October 14, 2015, *http://fortune.com/2015/10/14 /gopro-entertainment-empire/.*

25. Marshall W. Van Alstyne, Geoffrey G. Parker, and Sangeet Paul Choudary, "6 Reasons Platforms Fail," *Harvard Business Review*, March 31, 2016, *https://hbr.org/2016/03/6-reasons-platforms-fail.*

26. Ibid.

27. Elizabeth Jensen, "NPR Website To Get Rid Of Comments," NPR, August 11, 2016, *www.npr.org/sections/ombudsman/2016/08/17/489516952 /npr-website-to-get-rid-of-comments.*

Chapter 6

1. "Google's ad revenue from 2001 to 2016," *Statista, www.statista.com /statistics/266249/advertising-revenue-of-google/*.
2. Eric Schmidt and Jonathan Rosenberg, *How Google Works* (New York: Grand Central Publishing, 2014), 18–19.
3. Ibid., 19–20.
4. "Employee Engagement," *Gallup, www.gallup.com/Search/Default.aspx?s= &p=1&q=employee+engadgment&b=Go*.
5. Richard Branson, *The Virgin Way: If It's Not Fun, It's Not Worth Doing* (New York: Portfolio Publishing, 2015), 94–95.
6. Ibid., 120.
7. Richard Branson, "Virgin's Richard Branson: Apple boss Steve Jobs was the entrepreneur I most admired," *The Telegraph*, October 6, 2011, *www .telegraph.co.uk/technology/steve-jobs/8811232/Virgins-Richard-Branson -Apple-boss-Steve-Jobs-was-the-entrepreneur-I-most-admired.html*.
8. "Why GE is giving up employee ratings, abandoning annual reviews and rethinking the role of HQ," *LinkedIn*, August 4, 2016, *www.linkedin.com/pulse/ why-ge-giving-up-employee-ratings-abandoning-annual-reviews-immelt*.
9. Lisa Earle McLeod, *Leading with Noble Purpose* (Gildan Media, 2017).
10. "Millennials want business to shift its purpose," *Deloitte, www2.deloitte. com/au/en/pages/about-deloitte/articles/millennial-survey-2016-shifting -business-purpose.html#*.
11. McLeod and More, accessed March 14, 2017, *www.mcleodandmore.com/*.
12. David Rock and Heidi Grant, "Why Diverse Teams Are Smarter," *Harvard Business Review*, November 4, 2016.
13. Matt Egan, "Workers tell Wells Fargo horror stories," *CNN Money*, September 9, 2016, *http://money.cnn.com/2016/09/09/investing/wells-fargo -phony-accounts-culture/index.html?iid=EL*.
14. Billy Medof, speaker at Setili & Associates Strategic Agility Think Tank event, May 24, 2016.
15. "Heart Disease, Stroke and Research Statistics At-a-Glance," *American Heart Association*, December 16, 2015.
16. Gina Kolata, "A Sea Change in Treating Heart Attacks," *New York Times*, June 19, 2015, *www.nytimes.com/2015/06/21/health/saving-heart-attack -victims-stat.html?_r=0*.
17. Jay Greene, "Look Who's Back! Microsoft, Rebooted, Emerges as a Tech Leader," *The Wall Street Journal*, December 16, 2016, *www.wsj.com/articles /look-whos-back-microsoft-rebooted-emerges-as-a-tech-leader-1481900876*.
18. Michael Tushman, "Leadership Tips for Today to Stay in the Game Tomorrow," *IESE Insight* 23, 24.
19. Max Nisen, "Why GE had to kill its annual performance reviews after more than three decades," *Quartz*, August 13, 2015.
20. "Joy, Engagement and Creativity at Work" (Boston: Harvard Business Review Press, 2011), 81.
21. John Dowdy and Kirk Rieckhoff, "Agility in U.S. National Security." McKinsey & Co., March 2017, *www.mckinsey.com/industries/public-sector /our-insights/agility-in-us-national-security*.

22. "New Citi/LinkedIn Survey Reveals Men Struggle with Work-Life Balance—But May Not Be Telling Women Their Concerns," *Citi*, October 28, 2015, *www.citigroup.com/citi/news/2014/141028a.htm.*
23. Ashton Morrow, "Delta Cargo President: 'Leadership must always be humble'," *Delta News Hub*, June 3, 2016, *http://news.delta.com /delta-cargo-president-leadership-must-always-be-humble.*
24. Ibid.

Chapter 7

1. Adam Lashinsky, "The Unexpected Management Genius of Facebook's Mark Zuckerberg," *Fortune*, November 10, 2016, *http://fortune.com/facebook -mark-zuckerberg-business/.*
2. "How to win friends and influence people," *The Economist*, April 9, 2016, *www.economist.com/news/briefing/21696507-social-network-has-turned -itself-one-worlds-most-influential-technology-giants.*
3. Ibid.
4. Thomas Friedman, *Thank You for Being Late: An Optimist's Guide to Thriving in the Age of Accelerations* (New York: Farrar, Straus and Giroux, 2016).
5. Alan Weiss, *The Great Big Book of Process Visuals* (East Greenwich, R.I.: Las Brisas Research Press, 2003).
6. Jay Greene, "Look Who's Back! Microsoft, Rebooted, Emerges as a Tech Leader," *The Wall Street Journal*, December 17, 2016.
7. "UPS Fact Sheet," *UPS*, 2016, *www.pressroom.ups.com/pressroom/Content DetailsViewer.page?ConceptType=FactSheets&id=1426321563187-193*
8. Rimas Kapeskas, managing director of the UPS Strategic Enterprise Fund, speaking at Setili & Associates Strategic Agility Think Tank, October 14, 2016.
9. Ben Veghte, "PitchBook Named the Official Data Provider of NVCA," *National Venture Capital Association*, September 21, 2016, *http://nvca.org /pressreleases_category/corporate-venture/*
10. Tim Peterson, "Facebook's Mobile Revenue Climbs to $2.5 Billion as Ad Prices Soar," *AdvertisingAge*, January 28, 2015, *http://adage.com/article /digital/facebook-s-mobile-revenue-hits-2-5-billion-prices-soar/296869/.*

Chapter 8

1. Marvin Riley, interview, March 11, 2017.
2. Jim Connell, interview, February 7, 2017.
3. Steve Macadam, interview, February 1, 2017.
4. Paul J. Zak, "The Neuroscience of Trust," *Harvard Business Review*, January–February 2017, *https://hbr.org/2017/01/the-neuroscience-of-trust.*
5. Karyn Twaronite, "A Global Survey on the Ambiguous State of Employee Trust," *Harvard Business Review*, July 22, 2016, *https://hbr .org/2016/07/a-global-survey-on-the-ambiguous-state-of-employee-trust.*
6. "Building Trust 2013: Workforce Trends Defining High Performance," *Interaction Associates and Human Capital Institute* (2013): 2.
7. Ibid., 14.

8. Stephen M.R. Covey, *The Speed of Trust: The One Thing That Changes Everything* (New York: Free Press, 2008), 13.
9. Luke Johnson, "Trust can seem risky but its absence is perilous," *Financial Times*, December 2, 2014, *www.ft.com/content/e2ac0cee-7948-11e4-9567-00144feabdc0*.
10. Shana Lebowitz, "Google considers this to be the most critical trait of successful teams," *Business Insider*, November 20, 2015, *www.businessinsider.com/amy-edmondson-on-psychological-safety-2015-11*.
11. Amy Edmondson, "Building a psychologically safe workplace: on Amy Edmondson at TEDxHGSE," *YouTube*, May 4, 2014, *https://youtu.be/LhoLuui9gX8*.
12. Paul J. Zak, "The Neuroscience of Trust," *Harvard Business Review*, January–February 2017, *https://hbr.org/2017/01/the-neuroscience-of-trust*.
13. Jim Connell, interview, February 7, 2017.
14. Patrick Lencioni, *The Five Dysfunctions of the Team* (New York: Jossey-Bass, 2007).
15. Michael Tushman, Wendy Smith, and Andy Binns, "The Ambidextrous CEO," *Harvard Business Review* (2011): 76.
16. "AmazonJobs," *www.amazon.jobs/principles*.
17. Billy Medof, speaker at Setili & Associates Strategic Agility Think Tank event, May 24, 2016.
18. Stephen M.R. Covey, *The Speed of Trust: The One Thing That Changes Everything* (New York: Free Press, 2008).

Chapter 9

1. Patrick McGee, "SAP aims to pull Europe out of 'digital recession,'" *Financial Times*, January 25, 2017.
2. "OCEARCH Lowcountry Expedition Education Packet," OCEARCH, *www.ocearch.org/expeditions/wp-content/uploads/2017/03/LowcountryExpeditionPacket-2.pdf*.
3. Richard Branson, *The Virgin Way: If It's Not Fun, It's Not Worth Doing* (Portfolio Publishing, 2015), 211.
4. Ed Bastian, with Kai Ryssdal on "Marketplace," reported on Delta News Hub website, *http://news.delta.com/bastian-marketplace-my-job-taking-care-our-people*.

INDEX

251

ACKNOWLEDGMENTS

Thank you to all my clients and Strategic Agility Think Tank community members who contributed ideas, examples, and inspiration as I wrote this book. These include Amy Mills and Joe George (Cox Automotive); Dan Csont, Beverley Reid, and Kristen Shovlin (Delta Air Lines); Kimberly Williams (Diageo); Jim Connell, Marvin Riley, and Steve Macadam (EnPro Industries); Andy Bodea, Scott Waid, Jonathan Siskin, Isio Nelson, Shawn Holtzclaw, Patricia Rosenfeld, and Ramesh Subramaniam (Equifax); Mitch Free (Fast Radius); Jeff Fleck and Billy Medof (Georgia-Pacific); Dana Hudson, Brandon Hayes, and John Kelsch (The Home Depot); Jay Caiafa (IHG); Rob Frohwein (Kabbage); John Morrow and Eli Rosner (NCR); Grady Grant (Mead Johnson Nutrition); Hala Moddelmog (Metro Atlanta Chamber); Chris Fischer (OCEARCH); Brian Caldarelli, Brandi Quinn, and Deanna Williams (PSCU); Marcell Vollmer (SAP); Cheryl Lester (Walmart); and Jan Willem Breen, David Lee, and Rimas Kapeskas (UPS).

Thank you to my developmental editor, Peter Economy. He is a wise, creative, and generous thought partner and guide.

Thank you to Alan Weiss, for helping me to shape my ideas and offering advice at many steps along the way, for many years. And thank you to my colleagues in Alan's community, including Andy

Bass, Connie Dieken, Lisa Earle McLeod, Lorraine Moore, Rick Pay, and Val Wright, who generously shared their expertise and guidance. Thank you to Mark Levy, for helping me to realize how fascinating writing can be.

Thank you to the team at Career Press, including Michael Pye, Adam Schwartz, Jeff Piasky, Gina Schenck, and Lauren Manoy, for seeing the promise in my book and bringing it to fruition.

Thank you to Amy Edmondson, Teresa Amabile, Frank Cespedes, and Michael Tushman at Harvard Business School for their contributions.

Thank you to Nelson Chu and others for building a vibrant and long-lived Atlanta McKinsey alumni community, a source of many valued friendships and ideas.

Thank you to Marshall Goldsmith, for contributing a foreword, and for being an inspiring and generous role model.

Thank you to my daughters, Alison and Lee, who provide me with ideas and perspectives that keep me fresh. Thank you to my mother, Nancy Keahey, who provides me with the wisdom of history while still being a thoroughly modern thinker.

Thank you to my husband, Rob, who gave me new ideas, examples, and insight daily, and creates the fun, travel, and adventure in our lives.